The Basics of Healthy Eating: A Beginner's Guide.

RYBAIEV VOLODYMYR

The Basics of Healthy Eating: A Beginner's Guide.

The Basics of Healthy Eating: A Beginner's Guide.

Table of contents

Introduction: 4
Fundamentals of Healthy Eating 6
   Variety of Food Groups 6
      Grains and their significance 6
      Fruits and Vegetables in Your Diet 8
      Protein Sources and Plant-Based Alternatives 10
      Dairy Products and Their Alternatives 12
      Healthy Fats and Oils 14
   Moderation in Food Consumption 16
      Portion Sizes and Portion Control 16
      Healthy Snacking and Choosing Snacks Wisely 18
      Regularity of Meals 20
      Managing Hunger and Appetite 22
   Hydration and Drinking Habits 24
      Importance of Adequate Hydration 24
      Choosing Healthy Beverages 27
      Avoiding Sugary and Carbonated Drinks 30
Nutrition and Health 32
   Healthy Eating for Disease Prevention 32
      Cardiovascular Health 32
      Obesity and Diabetes Prevention 35
      Bone and Dental Health 38
      Boosting Immunity and Overall Well-Being 41
   The Role of Healthy Eating in Mental Health 44
      Impact of Nutrition on Mood and Emotional Well-Being 44
      Nutrition for Improved Focus and Memory 47
      Wholesome Snacks and Desserts 50
Practical Tips and Recommendations 53

- Meal Planning and Menu Creation 53
  - Weekly Meal Planning 53
  - Grocery Shopping and Selecting Quality Ingredients 56
  - Food Preparation and Storage 59
- Various Dietary Approaches 62
  - Vegetarianism and Veganism 62
  - Paleo and Ketogenic Diets 65
  - Gluten and Lactose Intolerance 67
- Handy Collection of Healthy Recipes 70
  - Nutritious Breakfast Options 70
  - Healthy Lunches and Dinners 73
  - Wholesome Snacks and Desserts 76

Sustaining Healthy Eating in Everyday Life 79
- Overcoming Challenges and Temptations 79
  - Dealing with Cravings and Overeating 79
  - Mindful Eating and Mindful Food Choices 82
  - Handling Social Situations and Events 85
- Healthy Eating on the Go 88
  - Choosing Healthy Options at Restaurants and Cafes 88
  - Eating Well During Travel and Business Trips 91
  - Packing Nutritious Meals for Work and School 94

Conclusion 97
- Recap and Key Principles of Healthy Eating 97
- Inspiration and Motivation for Sustaining a Healthy Lifestyle ... 99

The Basics of Healthy Eating: A Beginner's Guide.

Introduction:

Welcome to "The Basics of Healthy Eating: A Beginner's Guide." In this book, we will embark on a journey towards understanding and embracing the principles of healthy eating, with a focus on providing valuable guidance to beginners who are eager to improve their nutrition and well-being.

In today's fast-paced world, where convenience often takes precedence over conscious choices, it's easy to neglect our dietary needs. However, healthy eating is not a mere trend or passing fad; it is a fundamental pillar of overall health and vitality. By nourishing our bodies with the right foods, we can unlock an abundance of benefits, ranging from increased energy levels and improved mood to enhanced disease prevention and longevity.

The purpose of this book is to provide you with the essential knowledge and practical tools you need to embark on a journey of healthy eating. We will explore the key principles of nutrition, delve into the various food groups, and learn how to make informed choices when it comes to selecting and preparing meals. Whether you're a busy professional, a student, or a parent looking to provide the best for your family, this guide is designed to empower you to make positive changes in your diet and lifestyle.

Throughout the pages of this book, we will address the importance of incorporating a variety of food groups into your meals, emphasizing the significance of grains, fruits, vegetables, proteins, dairy alternatives, and healthy fats. We will delve into the concept of moderation, guiding you on portion control, healthy snacking, and establishing a regular eating routine. Furthermore, we will explore the crucial role of hydration and provide tips for choosing beverages that support your overall well-being.

But healthy eating is not only about physical health; it also profoundly impacts our mental and emotional well-being. We will examine how nutrition influences our mood, cognitive function, and sleep patterns, equipping you with knowledge to optimize these aspects of your life through mindful food choices.

This book will go beyond theory and provide you with practical recommendations and strategies to implement healthy eating in your daily life. From meal planning and grocery shopping to cooking and storing food, you will learn how to navigate the challenges and create a sustainable routine that supports your goals.

So, whether you are just starting your journey towards healthy eating or seeking to deepen your understanding of nutrition, this guide is here to serve as a trusted companion. Together, let's unlock the secrets of healthy eating and embrace a lifestyle that nourishes both body and mind.

Are you ready to embark on this exciting adventure? Let's dive into the foundations of healthy eating and discover a world of delicious possibilities that will transform the way you approach food and your overall well-being.

Fundamentals of Healthy Eating

Variety of Food Groups

Grains and their significance

Grains form an essential part of a healthy and balanced diet. They are one of the key food groups that provide us with essential nutrients, energy, and fiber. In this chapter, we will explore the significance of grains and how they contribute to our overall well-being.

Understanding Grains:
Grains, also known as cereals, are the seeds of grass-like plants that are cultivated for food. They come in various forms, including wheat, rice, oats, barley, corn, and rye. Grains are versatile and can be processed into different products like bread, pasta, cereals, and flours.

Nutritional Value:
Grains are rich in carbohydrates, which serve as the primary source of energy for our bodies. They also provide dietary fiber, vitamins, minerals, and phytochemicals that are vital for optimal health. Whole grains, in particular, are exceptionally nutritious as they retain the bran, germ, and endosperm, whereas refined grains have had the bran and germ removed, resulting in a loss of valuable nutrients.

Health Benefits of Grains:
a. Energy and Satiety: The carbohydrates in grains provide the energy needed for our daily activities. Additionally, the fiber content in whole grains promotes satiety and helps regulate appetite, aiding in weight management.
b. Digestive Health: The fiber in grains supports a healthy digestive system by preventing constipation, promoting regular bowel movements, and feeding beneficial gut bacteria.
c. Heart Health: Whole grains have been linked to a reduced risk of heart disease. They contain soluble fiber, which helps lower cholesterol levels, and other heart-healthy compounds like antioxidants and phytochemicals.

d. Blood Sugar Control: Whole grains have a lower glycemic index, which means they cause a slower and steadier rise in blood sugar levels compared to refined grains. This makes them beneficial for individuals with diabetes or those aiming to prevent it.

e. Nutrient Profile: Grains are a good source of B vitamins, including thiamin, riboflavin, niacin, and folate. These vitamins play essential roles in energy production, brain function, and the formation of red blood cells.

Choosing and Incorporating Grains:

a. Whole Grains: Opt for whole grains whenever possible. Look for whole wheat, brown rice, quinoa, oats, and other intact grains that retain their natural goodness.

b. Reading Labels: When purchasing grain-based products, read the ingredient list carefully. Choose items that list whole grains as the first ingredient and avoid those that contain refined grains or excessive added sugars.

c. Diverse Options: Explore a variety of grains to diversify your nutrient intake and add excitement to your meals. Experiment with lesser-known grains like amaranth, millet, or farro to expand your culinary horizons.

d. Portion Control: Pay attention to portion sizes to ensure a balanced intake of grains. Aim for about half of your grain servings to be whole grains while the other half can include refined grains in moderation.

Incorporating grains into your diet is an integral part of healthy eating. By opting for whole grains and understanding their nutritional significance, you can enjoy their many health benefits and promote overall well-being. In the next chapter, we will explore the importance of incorporating fruits and vegetables into your diet for a well-rounded approach to healthy eating.

Fruits and Vegetables in Your Diet

In this chapter, we will delve into the importance of incorporating fruits and vegetables into your daily diet. Fruits and vegetables are nature's powerhouses of essential nutrients, vitamins, minerals, and antioxidants that are crucial for maintaining good health. Let's explore their significance and how you can maximize their benefits.

Nutritional Powerhouses:
Fruits and vegetables are nutrient-dense foods that offer a wide array of vitamins, minerals, and dietary fiber. They are low in calories and high in water content, making them an excellent choice for maintaining a healthy weight. Consuming a variety of fruits and vegetables provides your body with essential nutrients such as vitamin C, vitamin A, potassium, folate, and dietary fiber.

Disease Prevention:
Numerous studies have shown that a diet rich in fruits and vegetables can help reduce the risk of chronic diseases, including heart disease, certain cancers, and type 2 diabetes. The natural antioxidants found in fruits and vegetables help protect the body against oxidative stress and inflammation, both of which are linked to the development of these diseases.

Fiber and Digestive Health:
Fruits and vegetables are excellent sources of dietary fiber, which plays a vital role in maintaining a healthy digestive system. Fiber aids in preventing constipation, promotes regular bowel movements, and supports a diverse and thriving gut microbiome. Additionally, fiber contributes to a feeling of fullness, which can help with weight management.

Variety and Color:
To reap the maximum benefits, it is important to consume a diverse range of fruits and vegetables. Different fruits and vegetables offer unique combinations of vitamins, minerals, and phytochemicals. Aim for a colorful plate by incorporating a wide range of fruits and vegetables of various hues, including leafy greens, vibrant berries, citrus fruits, cruciferous vegetables, and more.

Tips for Incorporating Fruits and Vegetables:

a. Fresh and Seasonal: Opt for fresh, locally grown fruits and vegetables whenever possible. Seasonal produce tends to be more flavorful and nutrient-rich.

b. Snack Smart: Keep cut-up fruits and vegetables on hand for convenient and healthy snacking. Pair them with a nutritious dip or spread like hummus or nut butter for added flavor.

c. Variety of Preparation Methods: Experiment with different cooking techniques such as steaming, roasting, grilling, or stir-frying to bring out the natural flavors and textures of fruits and vegetables.

d. Smoothies and Juices: Blend fruits and vegetables into smoothies or juices for a refreshing and nutritious beverage. However, be mindful of added sugars and opt for whole fruits or vegetables whenever possible to retain the dietary fiber.

e. Fill Half Your Plate: Aim to fill at least half of your plate with a colorful assortment of fruits and vegetables at each meal.

By making fruits and vegetables a prominent part of your diet, you can support your overall health and well-being. In the next chapter, we will explore the importance of protein and its role in maintaining a balanced and healthy diet.

The Basics of Healthy Eating: A Beginner's Guide.

Protein Sources and Plant-Based Alternatives

Protein is an essential nutrient that plays a vital role in numerous functions within our bodies. In this chapter, we will explore the significance of protein, different sources of protein, and plant-based alternatives that can meet your dietary needs.

Importance of Protein:
Proteins are the building blocks of our bodies, responsible for the growth, repair, and maintenance of tissues, muscles, enzymes, hormones, and immune cells. Consuming an adequate amount of protein is crucial for supporting overall health, promoting satiety, and aiding in weight management.

Animal-Based Protein Sources:
Animal products are well-known sources of protein and offer complete proteins that contain all the essential amino acids our bodies need. Some common animal-based protein sources include:
a. Lean meats (chicken, turkey, beef, pork)
b. Fish and seafood (salmon, tuna, shrimp)
c. Eggs and dairy products (milk, cheese, yogurt)
d. Poultry (chicken, turkey)

Plant-Based Protein Sources:
Plant-based protein sources are an excellent option for individuals following a vegetarian or vegan diet or those looking to reduce their consumption of animal products. While plant-based proteins are often incomplete, combining different plant-based protein sources can provide all the essential amino acids. Some plant-based protein sources include:
a. Legumes and beans (lentils, chickpeas, black beans)
b. Soy products (tofu, tempeh, edamame)
c. Nuts and seeds (almonds, walnuts, chia seeds)
d. Whole grains (quinoa, brown rice, oats)
e. Vegetables (spinach, broccoli, peas)

Plant-Based Alternatives:
For those seeking alternatives to animal-based proteins, there are numerous plant-based protein alternatives available in the market today. These alternatives are often made from soy, peas, or other

plant-based sources and can mimic the taste and texture of animal-based proteins. Some common plant-based protein alternatives include:
a. Plant-based meat substitutes (veggie burgers, plant-based sausages)
b. Plant-based dairy alternatives (soy milk, almond milk)
c. Tofu and tempeh as alternatives to meat or poultry
d. Plant-based protein powders (pea protein, hemp protein)

Combining Plant-Based Proteins:
To ensure you obtain all the essential amino acids, it's important to combine different plant-based protein sources. For example, pairing legumes with grains (e.g., beans with rice) creates a complete protein profile. Additionally, incorporating a variety of plant-based protein sources throughout the day can help meet your protein needs.

Considerations for Plant-Based Diets:
If you follow a plant-based diet, it's essential to pay attention to other nutrients that may be lacking, such as vitamin B12, iron, and omega-3 fatty acids. Consider incorporating fortified foods or supplements to ensure you meet your nutritional requirements.

By incorporating both animal-based and plant-based protein sources into your diet, you can ensure an adequate intake of this vital nutrient. Plant-based alternatives offer a variety of options for individuals looking to reduce their reliance on animal products or embrace a vegetarian or vegan lifestyle. In the next chapter, we will explore the role of dairy products and their alternatives in a healthy eating plan.

Dairy Products and Their Alternatives

Dairy products have long been a prominent part of many people's diets, providing a rich source of essential nutrients. However, for various reasons, some individuals may opt for dairy alternatives. In this chapter, we will explore dairy products, their nutritional value, and alternative options for those seeking non-dairy alternatives.

Nutritional Value of Dairy Products:
Dairy products, such as milk, cheese, and yogurt, are known for their high calcium content, which is essential for strong bones and teeth. They also provide protein, vitamins (such as vitamin D and B12), minerals (like phosphorus and potassium), and beneficial bacteria (in fermented dairy products).

Dairy Alternatives:
For individuals who are lactose intolerant, have milk allergies, or choose to follow a vegan lifestyle, there is a wide range of dairy alternatives available. These alternatives are typically plant-based and offer comparable nutrients. Some popular dairy alternatives include:
a. Plant-based milks: Soy milk, almond milk, coconut milk, oat milk, and rice milk.
b. Non-dairy yogurts: Soy yogurt, almond yogurt, coconut yogurt, and oat yogurt.
c. Cheese alternatives: Nut-based cheeses, soy cheese, and coconut-based cheese substitutes.

Nutritional Considerations for Dairy Alternatives:
While dairy alternatives can provide similar taste and texture, it's important to consider their nutritional composition. Some alternatives are fortified with nutrients like calcium, vitamin D, and B vitamins to mimic the nutritional profile of dairy products. However, others may be lower in protein or lack certain micronutrients, so it's important to read labels and choose options that meet your specific dietary needs.

Making Informed Choices:
When opting for dairy alternatives, consider the following:

a. Read Labels: Look for options that are fortified with essential nutrients and have limited added sugars.
b. Protein Content: Some dairy alternatives, like soy milk and pea protein-based products, offer a higher protein content than others. Choose alternatives that provide a sufficient amount of protein if it is a dietary concern.
c. Taste and Texture: Experiment with different brands and types of dairy alternatives to find the ones that best suit your preferences.

Calcium and Vitamin D:
Dairy products are a significant source of calcium and vitamin D. If you choose to consume dairy alternatives, ensure that you are obtaining these essential nutrients through other dietary sources or fortified alternatives. Leafy green vegetables, fortified plant-based milks, and calcium supplements can help meet your calcium needs. Exposure to sunlight and fortified foods can provide vitamin D.

Personalized Approach:
The choice between dairy products and their alternatives ultimately depends on individual preferences, dietary restrictions, and health considerations. It's essential to find a balance that suits your needs and ensures you meet your nutritional requirements.

By considering dairy alternatives and choosing those that align with your dietary needs and preferences, you can still enjoy a wide range of delicious and nutritious options. In the next chapter, we will explore the importance of incorporating healthy fats and oils into your diet for overall well-being.

The Basics of Healthy Eating: A Beginner's Guide.

Healthy Fats and Oils

Fats and oils play a crucial role in our diet, providing essential nutrients and contributing to overall health and well-being. In this chapter, we will explore the importance of incorporating healthy fats and oils into your diet and how they can support your body's needs.

Understanding Fats:
Fats are an essential macronutrient that provides energy, aids in nutrient absorption, and helps maintain cell function. It's important to note that not all fats are created equal. While some fats are beneficial for our health, others should be consumed in moderation.

Different Types of Fats:
a. Monounsaturated Fats: Found in foods such as avocados, olives, nuts, and seeds, monounsaturated fats are considered heart-healthy fats. They can help lower bad cholesterol levels and reduce the risk of heart disease when consumed in moderation.
b. Polyunsaturated Fats: Sources of polyunsaturated fats include fatty fish (salmon, trout), flaxseeds, chia seeds, walnuts, and certain oils (sunflower, soybean, and corn oils). These fats contain essential omega-3 and omega-6 fatty acids, which are important for brain function, heart health, and reducing inflammation.
c. Saturated Fats: Found in animal products like meat and dairy, as well as some plant-based oils like coconut oil and palm oil, saturated fats should be consumed in moderation. A high intake of saturated fats may increase cholesterol levels and the risk of heart disease.
d. Trans Fats: Artificially produced trans fats (partially hydrogenated oils) should be avoided as much as possible. Trans fats are found in processed foods, fried snacks, and some baked goods. They can increase bad cholesterol levels and raise the risk of heart disease.

Role of Healthy Fats and Oils:
a. Nutrient Absorption: Healthy fats play a vital role in the absorption of fat-soluble vitamins (vitamins A, D, E, and K) and other important nutrients.

b. Energy and Satiety: Fats are a concentrated source of energy and can help provide a feeling of fullness and satisfaction after meals.
c. Heart Health: Consuming adequate amounts of monounsaturated and polyunsaturated fats in place of saturated and trans fats can help improve heart health by reducing bad cholesterol levels and inflammation.
d. Brain Function: Omega-3 fatty acids, specifically DHA and EPA, are essential for brain health and cognitive function. Including sources like fatty fish and walnuts in your diet can support brain health.
e. Cell Structure: Fats are crucial for the structure and function of cell membranes, aiding in proper cell signaling and overall cellular health.

Incorporating Healthy Fats and Oils:
a. Plant-Based Oils: Opt for healthier plant-based oils, such as olive oil, canola oil, and avocado oil, for cooking, baking, and salad dressings. These oils are rich in monounsaturated fats and offer numerous health benefits.
b. Fatty Fish: Include fatty fish like salmon, mackerel, and sardines in your diet a few times a week to obtain omega-3 fatty acids.
c. Nuts and Seeds: Snack on a variety of nuts and seeds, such as almonds, walnuts, chia seeds, and flaxseeds, which provide healthy fats and other beneficial nutrients.
d. Moderation with Saturated Fats: Limit the intake of saturated fats by choosing lean cuts of meat, low-fat dairy products, and opting for healthier cooking methods like grilling or baking instead of frying.
e. Avoiding Trans Fats: Read food labels and avoid products that contain partially hydrogenated oils, as these often indicate the presence of trans fats.

By incorporating a balance of healthy fats and oils into your diet, you can support overall health, promote heart health, and ensure proper nutrient absorption. In the next chapter, we will discuss the importance of hydration and choosing healthy beverages to support your well-being.

Moderation in Food Consumption

Portion Sizes and Portion Control

Portion sizes and portion control are essential aspects of maintaining a healthy diet and managing weight. In this chapter, we will explore the importance of portion sizes, how they impact our overall health, and strategies for practicing portion control.

Understanding Portion Sizes:
Portion sizes refer to the amount of food we choose to eat at a given time. It is important to differentiate between portion sizes and serving sizes. A serving size is a standardized measurement recommended by health professionals, while portion sizes can vary based on individual preferences and eating habits.

Impact of Portion Sizes on Health:
Overconsumption of large portion sizes has been linked to weight gain, obesity, and various health issues. Larger portions often lead to increased calorie intake, making it more challenging to maintain a healthy weight and meet nutritional needs.

Practicing Portion Control:
a. Mindful Eating: Pay attention to your body's hunger and fullness cues. Eat slowly, savoring each bite, and stop eating when you feel comfortably satisfied, rather than overly full.
b. Use Smaller Plates and Bowls: Opt for smaller plates and bowls to create the illusion of a fuller plate and reduce the likelihood of overeating.
c. Measure and Weigh Foods: Use measuring cups, spoons, and kitchen scales to accurately portion out your food, especially when starting out. This practice can help you become more aware of appropriate serving sizes.
d. Fill Half Your Plate with Vegetables: By filling half of your plate with vegetables, you can naturally limit the portion sizes of higher-calorie foods while ensuring a balanced and nutrient-rich meal.
e. Be Mindful of High-Calorie Foods: Pay extra attention to portion sizes of calorie-dense foods such as oils, nuts, and sweets. Enjoy them in moderation and consider using smaller containers or portioning them out in advance.

f. Pre-Portion Snacks: Instead of eating directly from a large bag or container, pre-portion snacks into smaller, single-serving containers to avoid mindless eating and promote portion control.

g. Practice the Plate Method: Use the plate method as a guide for portion sizes: Fill half your plate with non-starchy vegetables, one-quarter with lean protein, and one-quarter with whole grains or starchy vegetables.

h. Seek Nutritional Guidance: Consult with a registered dietitian or nutritionist to receive personalized guidance on appropriate portion sizes and to develop a meal plan that suits your specific needs.

Balancing Macronutrients:
In addition to portion sizes, it's important to consider the balance of macronutrients in your meals. Aim to include a balance of carbohydrates, proteins, and healthy fats in appropriate portion sizes to ensure a well-rounded and satisfying meal.

Mindful Eating Habits:
Practicing mindful eating can go hand in hand with portion control. By paying attention to your eating habits, savoring each bite, and being aware of physical hunger and fullness cues, you can develop a healthier relationship with food and maintain appropriate portion sizes naturally.

Remember, portion control is about finding the right balance for your body and lifestyle. By adopting mindful eating practices and implementing portion control strategies, you can support your health, manage your weight, and enjoy a balanced and satisfying diet. In the next chapter, we will explore the importance of regular and balanced meal timing for optimal nutrition.

Healthy Snacking and Choosing Snacks Wisely

Snacking can be an important part of a balanced diet, providing energy and nutrients between meals. In this chapter, we will explore the significance of healthy snacking, strategies for choosing snacks wisely, and nutritious snack options to support your overall well-being.

The Importance of Healthy Snacking:
Healthy snacking can offer several benefits, including:
a. Managing Hunger: Snacks can help bridge the gap between meals and prevent excessive hunger, which can lead to overeating.
b. Providing Energy: Nutritious snacks can provide a boost of energy, particularly during periods of increased activity or when there is a long gap between meals.
c. Supporting Nutrient Intake: Well-chosen snacks can contribute to meeting your daily nutritional requirements, ensuring a balanced diet.

Strategies for Choosing Snacks Wisely:
a. Nutrient Density: Opt for snacks that are nutrient-dense, providing essential vitamins, minerals, and fiber. Choose whole, minimally processed foods over highly processed options.
b. Portion Control: Be mindful of portion sizes when snacking. Pre-portion snacks into single-serving containers or use small plates and bowls to prevent overeating.
c. Balance Macronutrients: Include a combination of carbohydrates, proteins, and healthy fats in your snacks to provide sustained energy and promote satiety.
d. Read Labels: Pay attention to the ingredient list and nutritional information on packaged snacks. Look for options with minimal added sugars, sodium, and unhealthy fats.
e. Whole Foods: Emphasize whole foods as snacks, such as fruits, vegetables, nuts, seeds, and yogurt, which offer a wide range of nutrients without unnecessary additives.
f. Homemade Snacks: Consider preparing your own snacks at home using fresh ingredients. This allows you to control the quality and quantity of the ingredients.

g. Mindful Snacking: Practice mindful eating when snacking. Slow down, savor each bite, and pay attention to your body's hunger and fullness cues.

Nutritious Snack Options:
a. Fresh Fruits and Vegetables: Enjoy a variety of fresh, seasonal fruits and vegetables as snacks. They provide vitamins, minerals, fiber, and hydration.
b. Nuts and Seeds: Snack on a handful of almonds, walnuts, pumpkin seeds, or chia seeds, which offer healthy fats, protein, and fiber.
c. Greek Yogurt: Opt for plain, Greek yogurt and top it with fresh fruits or a sprinkle of nuts for added flavor and nutrition.
d. Whole Grain Crackers or Rice Cakes: Choose whole grain options as a base for spreads like hummus, nut butter, or avocado.
e. Homemade Trail Mix: Make your own trail mix by combining dried fruits, nuts, seeds, and a small portion of dark chocolate or whole-grain cereal.
f. Veggie Sticks with Dip: Snack on carrot sticks, celery, cucumber, or bell pepper slices paired with a healthy dip like hummus or Greek yogurt-based dips.
g. Hard-Boiled Eggs: Prepare hard-boiled eggs in advance and enjoy them as a protein-packed snack.
h. Smoothies: Blend fruits, vegetables, and a source of protein like Greek yogurt or plant-based protein powder for a nutritious and refreshing snack.

Remember, the key is to choose snacks that are satisfying, nutrient-dense, and align with your dietary goals. By practicing mindful snacking and opting for wholesome options, you can fuel your body with nutritious snacks that support your overall well-being. In the next chapter, we will explore the importance of regular meal timing and establishing a healthy eating routine.

Regularity of Meals

Establishing a regular eating routine and maintaining mealtime consistency can have a significant impact on overall health and well-being. In this chapter, we will explore the importance of regular meal timing, the benefits it offers, and strategies for incorporating regularity into your eating habits.

Importance of Regular Meal Timing:
Regular meal timing refers to maintaining consistent meal schedules throughout the day. This practice offers several benefits, including:
a. Enhanced Digestion: Regular meal timing allows your body to establish a rhythm, optimizing digestion and nutrient absorption.
b. Stable Energy Levels: Consistent meals provide a steady supply of energy throughout the day, preventing energy dips and promoting sustained focus and productivity.
c. Balanced Blood Sugar Levels: Regular meals help regulate blood sugar levels, preventing spikes and crashes that can affect energy, mood, and overall health.
d. Appetite Control: Eating at regular intervals can help regulate appetite, preventing excessive hunger or overeating.

Strategies for Establishing Regular Meal Timing:
a. Consistent Meal Schedule: Aim to eat meals at approximately the same times each day. Establish a routine that aligns with your daily schedule and allows for regular meal breaks.
b. Prioritize Breakfast: Make breakfast a priority to kick-start your metabolism and provide fuel for the day ahead. Aim to eat within an hour of waking up.
c. Plan and Prepare Meals in Advance: Plan your meals and snacks in advance, and if possible, prepare them ahead of time. This can help you adhere to a regular meal schedule and prevent impulsive, unhealthy food choices.
d. Mindful Eating: Sit down and focus on your meals, avoiding distractions such as screens or work. Eat slowly, savor each bite, and be mindful of your body's hunger and fullness cues.
e. Snack Strategically: If there is a long gap between meals, plan for nutritious snacks to maintain energy levels and prevent excessive hunger. Ensure your snacks align with your overall dietary goals.

f. Hydration: Stay adequately hydrated throughout the day by drinking water regularly. Dehydration can sometimes be mistaken for hunger, leading to irregular meal timing.

g. Be Flexible: While establishing a routine is beneficial, it's important to be flexible when necessary. Adapt your meal timing to accommodate changes in your schedule or special occasions, but strive to return to your regular routine as soon as possible.

Creating a Balanced Meal:
In addition to regular meal timing, focus on creating balanced meals that incorporate a variety of food groups. Include lean proteins, whole grains, fruits, vegetables, and healthy fats to ensure a well-rounded and nutritious diet.

Listen to Your Body:
While regular meal timing is important, it's also crucial to listen to your body's individual needs. Pay attention to hunger and fullness cues, and adjust your meal portions accordingly. Everyone's metabolism and energy requirements are unique, so be mindful of your body's signals.

By establishing regular meal timing and adhering to consistent eating routines, you can support optimal digestion, maintain stable energy levels, and promote overall health. In the next chapter, we will explore the significance of hydration and choosing healthy beverages for your well-being.

Managing Hunger and Appetite

Managing hunger and appetite is key to maintaining a balanced and healthy eating routine. In this chapter, we will explore strategies and techniques to help you effectively manage hunger, control appetite, and make mindful food choices.

Understanding Hunger and Appetite:
Hunger is the physical sensation that arises when your body needs nourishment and energy. Appetite, on the other hand, refers to the desire to eat, which can be influenced by various factors, including emotions, environmental cues, and learned behaviors.

Recognizing and Responding to Hunger:
a. Tune into Physical Signals: Pay attention to your body's physical cues, such as stomach growling, low energy, or a feeling of emptiness. These signs indicate that your body needs nourishment.
b. Mindful Eating: Practice mindful eating by slowing down and savoring each bite. This helps you become more aware of your body's hunger and fullness cues, allowing you to eat until you are comfortably satisfied.
c. Eat Balanced Meals: Ensure that your meals contain a balance of macronutrients (carbohydrates, proteins, and healthy fats) and fiber to promote satiety and provide sustained energy.

Strategies for Managing Hunger and Controlling Appetite:
a. Opt for Nutrient-Dense Foods: Choose whole, unprocessed foods that are rich in nutrients. Nutrient-dense foods tend to be more satisfying and can help curb cravings.
b. Prioritize Protein: Include protein-rich foods in your meals and snacks as they promote feelings of fullness and help regulate appetite. Good sources of protein include lean meats, fish, poultry, legumes, tofu, and Greek yogurt.
c. Fiber-Rich Foods: Incorporate fiber-rich foods, such as fruits, vegetables, whole grains, and legumes, into your meals. Fiber adds bulk to your meals and aids in digestion, keeping you feeling fuller for longer.
d. Stay Hydrated: Sometimes thirst can be mistaken for hunger. Drink water throughout the day to stay hydrated and minimize the likelihood of dehydration-induced hunger.

e. Mindful Snacking: When snacking, choose nutrient-dense options that provide both satisfaction and nourishment. Opt for a combination of protein, healthy fats, and fiber to promote satiety.
f. Emotional Eating Awareness: Be mindful of emotional triggers that may lead to eating when not truly hungry. Find alternative ways to cope with emotions, such as engaging in physical activity, practicing relaxation techniques, or seeking support from friends or professionals.
g. Stress Management: Implement stress-reducing techniques like meditation, yoga, or engaging in hobbies to help prevent stress-related eating.
h. Sleep Well: Prioritize getting enough quality sleep as lack of sleep can disrupt hunger-regulating hormones, leading to increased appetite and cravings.
i. Regular Physical Activity: Engage in regular physical activity, as it can help regulate appetite, improve mood, and promote overall well-being.

Portion Control and Mindful Eating:
Practice portion control by being mindful of the quantity of food you consume. Use smaller plates and bowls, measure ingredients, and be aware of appropriate portion sizes. Eating slowly and paying attention to the taste and texture of your food can also aid in recognizing satiety.

Remember that managing hunger and appetite is a personal journey. Listen to your body, be mindful of your eating patterns, and adopt strategies that work best for you. By doing so, you can maintain a healthy relationship with food and support your overall well-being. In the next chapter, we will explore the impact of nutrition on cardiovascular health.

Hydration and Drinking Habits

Importance of Adequate Hydration

Hydration is vital for maintaining overall health and well-being. In this chapter, we will explore the importance of adequate hydration, the benefits it offers, and strategies for ensuring proper hydration.

Understanding the Importance of Hydration:
Water is essential for numerous bodily functions, including regulating body temperature, lubricating joints, delivering nutrients to cells, flushing waste from the body, and supporting proper organ function. Adequate hydration is crucial for optimal physical and cognitive performance.

Benefits of Adequate Hydration:
a. Optimal Physical Performance: Staying hydrated improves physical endurance, muscle function, and overall performance during exercise or physical activities.
b. Cognitive Function: Hydration is vital for maintaining mental clarity, concentration, and cognitive function. Even mild dehydration can negatively impact mood, memory, and cognitive performance.
c. Digestion and Nutrient Absorption: Water aids in digestion by breaking down food and facilitating nutrient absorption in the digestive tract.
d. Temperature Regulation: Proper hydration helps regulate body temperature, especially during physical exertion or in hot weather, preventing overheating and heat-related illnesses.
e. Joint and Muscle Health: Water acts as a lubricant for joints and helps cushion and protect muscles, reducing the risk of injuries and promoting mobility.
f. Skin Health: Good hydration contributes to healthy skin, preventing dryness and promoting a more youthful appearance.

Signs of Dehydration:
It is important to be aware of the signs of dehydration, which can include:
a. Thirst
b. Dry or sticky mouth

c. Fatigue or low energy
d. Dark-colored urine
e. Dry skin
f. Headaches or dizziness
g. Decreased urine output

Strategies for Maintaining Adequate Hydration:
a. Drink Enough Water: The Institute of Medicine recommends a daily water intake of about 2.7 liters (91 ounces) for women and 3.7 liters (125 ounces) for men. This can vary based on individual factors, activity levels, and climate.
b. Listen to Your Body: Pay attention to your body's thirst signals and drink water whenever you feel thirsty.
c. Sip Water Throughout the Day: Instead of relying on large quantities of water at once, sip water throughout the day to maintain consistent hydration levels.
d. Hydrate Before, During, and After Physical Activity: Drink water before, during, and after exercise or physical activity to replenish fluids lost through sweat.
e. Hydrate with Electrolytes: In cases of intense or prolonged physical activity or in hot weather, consider hydrating with electrolyte-rich beverages or foods to replenish essential minerals lost through sweat.
f. Include Hydrating Foods: Consume foods with high water content, such as fruits (watermelon, oranges, strawberries) and vegetables (cucumbers, lettuce, tomatoes), which can contribute to your overall hydration.
g. Limit Dehydrating Beverages: Limit or avoid beverages that can contribute to dehydration, such as sugary drinks, excessive caffeine, and alcohol.
h. Set Reminders: Use reminders or apps to help track and remind yourself to drink water regularly.
i. Consider Personal Factors: Individual hydration needs can vary based on factors like age, body weight, activity level, and climate. Adjust your fluid intake accordingly.

Proper hydration is essential for maintaining optimal health and functioning. By prioritizing adequate water intake and incorporating strategies to stay hydrated, you can support your overall well-being and promote optimal physical and cognitive performance. In the next chapter, we will explore the benefits of regular physical activity and its role in maintaining a healthy lifestyle.

Choosing Healthy Beverages

Beverage choices can have a significant impact on our overall health and well-being. In this chapter, we will explore the importance of choosing healthy beverages, the potential health risks associated with certain drinks, and strategies for making wise beverage choices.

The Significance of Healthy Beverage Choices:
Choosing healthy beverages is crucial for maintaining proper hydration, supporting nutrient intake, and promoting overall health. Beverages can contribute to our daily calorie intake, nutrient intake, and hydration status.

Hydration and Water:
Water is the optimal choice for staying hydrated. It has no calories, is essential for bodily functions, and plays a vital role in maintaining optimal health. Aim to drink plain water throughout the day and prioritize it as your primary beverage.

Beverage Guidelines and Limitations:
a. Sugary Drinks: Limit the consumption of sugary beverages such as soda, fruit juices, sweetened tea, sports drinks, and energy drinks. These drinks are typically high in added sugars and calories, and excessive consumption can contribute to weight gain, dental issues, and an increased risk of chronic diseases.
b. Caffeine: Moderate caffeine consumption from sources like coffee, tea, and some energy drinks. While moderate caffeine intake is generally considered safe for most individuals, excessive caffeine consumption can lead to side effects such as anxiety, disrupted sleep, and increased heart rate. It's best to limit intake and be mindful of individual tolerance.
c. Alcohol: Consume alcohol in moderation, if at all. Excessive alcohol consumption can have detrimental effects on health, including liver damage, increased risk of certain cancers, impaired judgment, and addiction. It's important to adhere to recommended guidelines for moderate alcohol intake or consider abstaining altogether.

Healthy Beverage Choices:

a. Water: As mentioned earlier, water should be the primary choice for hydration. It's calorie-free, readily available, and essential for maintaining proper bodily functions.
b. Herbal Tea: Enjoy a variety of herbal teas, such as chamomile, peppermint, or green tea. They provide hydration, antioxidants, and potential health benefits without added sugars or calories.
c. Infused Water: Add natural flavors to water by infusing it with fruits, vegetables, or herbs. This can enhance the taste and encourage increased water consumption.
d. Low-Fat Milk or Plant-Based Milk Alternatives: Incorporate low-fat dairy milk or plant-based milk alternatives fortified with nutrients like calcium and vitamin D into your diet. Choose unsweetened versions when possible.
e. Vegetable Juices: Enjoy vegetable juices made from fresh, whole vegetables without added sugars or sodium. These can be a nutritious way to increase vegetable intake, but be mindful of portion sizes.
f. Homemade Smoothies: Blend fresh or frozen fruits and vegetables with water or unsweetened milk alternatives to create nutritious smoothies. Be cautious of added sugars and control portion sizes.
g. Limited Fruit Juice: If you choose to consume fruit juice, opt for 100% juice without added sugars. However, it's best to consume whole fruits instead, as they provide more fiber and nutrients while limiting sugar intake.
h. Limit Sugary Drinks: Minimize or avoid sugary beverages such as soda, fruit punches, sweetened iced teas, and energy drinks. These are often high in added sugars and provide little to no nutritional value.

Reading Labels and Ingredient Lists:
When choosing beverages, read labels and ingredient lists to be aware of the sugar, calorie, and nutrient content. Pay attention to serving sizes and opt for options with minimal or no added sugars.

Remember to prioritize water as your primary beverage and make conscious choices when selecting other drinks. By choosing healthy beverages and limiting the consumption of sugary drinks, caffeine, and alcohol, you can support your overall health and hydration needs. In the next chapter, we will explore the benefits of regular physical activity and its role in maintaining a healthy lifestyle.

Avoiding Sugary and Carbonated Drinks

Eliminating or reducing the consumption of sugary and carbonated drinks can have a significant positive impact on your health. In this chapter, we will delve into the reasons why it's important to avoid these types of beverages and provide strategies for making healthier choices.

The Health Risks of Sugary and Carbonated Drinks:
a. Weight Gain and Obesity: Sugary drinks are high in calories and provide little to no nutritional value. Regular consumption of these beverages can contribute to weight gain and increase the risk of obesity.
b. Increased Risk of Chronic Diseases: Sugary drinks have been linked to an increased risk of chronic conditions such as type 2 diabetes, heart disease, and certain types of cancer.
c. Dental Issues: High sugar content in these beverages promotes tooth decay and cavities, leading to dental problems.
d. Blood Sugar Imbalances: Drinking sugary drinks can cause blood sugar spikes and subsequent crashes, impacting energy levels, mood, and overall well-being.
e. Poor Nutritional Value: Carbonated drinks and sugary beverages often lack essential nutrients and can displace healthier options in your diet.

Strategies for Avoiding Sugary and Carbonated Drinks:
a. Choose Water as Your Primary Beverage: Water is the healthiest and most hydrating choice. Make water your go-to option for quenching your thirst.
b. Flavor Water Naturally: Enhance the taste of water by adding natural flavors such as sliced fruits (lemon, lime, berries), cucumber, or herbs (mint, basil).
c. Opt for Unsweetened or Low-Sugar Alternatives: Choose unsweetened tea, herbal tea, or coffee. If you prefer a sweet taste, use natural sweeteners like stevia or a small amount of honey.
d. Drink Sparkling Water or Club Soda: If you enjoy the fizziness of carbonated drinks, opt for sparkling water or club soda without added sugars or artificial sweeteners.

e. Make Homemade Refreshing Beverages: Create your own refreshing beverages by infusing water with fruits, herbs, or even making homemade iced tea or fruit-infused water.
f. Read Labels and Choose Wisely: When purchasing beverages, read labels carefully. Avoid drinks with added sugars, high-fructose corn syrup, artificial sweeteners, or artificial flavors.
g. Be Mindful of Portion Sizes: If you occasionally choose sugary or carbonated drinks, practice moderation and be mindful of portion sizes. Opt for smaller cans or bottles and limit your intake.
h. Educate Yourself: Understand the detrimental effects of sugary and carbonated drinks on your health. Stay informed about the latest research and health recommendations regarding these beverages.

Find Healthy Alternatives:
a. Infused Water: Experiment with different combinations of fruits, vegetables, and herbs to create refreshing infused water.
b. Unsweetened Tea: Enjoy unsweetened herbal tea or green tea, which provide antioxidants and offer various health benefits.
c. Freshly Squeezed Juice: If you crave a fruity taste, opt for freshly squeezed juice with no added sugars. However, keep in mind that whole fruits are a healthier choice due to their fiber content.
d. Smoothies: Make your own smoothies using fresh or frozen fruits, vegetables, and a source of protein such as Greek yogurt or a plant-based protein powder. Avoid adding extra sugars.
e. Sparkling Water with a Twist: Choose sparkling water and add a splash of citrus juice or a few slices of your favorite fruit for flavor.

By avoiding sugary and carbonated drinks, you can reduce your intake of empty calories, added sugars, and artificial additives. Opting for healthier alternatives, such as water, infused water, unsweetened tea, or homemade beverages, supports your overall health and helps you maintain a balanced and nutritious diet. In the next chapter, we will explore the benefits of regular physical activity and its role in maintaining a healthy lifestyle.

Nutrition and Health

Healthy Eating for Disease Prevention

Cardiovascular Health

Maintaining cardiovascular health is essential for overall well-being and longevity. In this chapter, we will explore the importance of cardiovascular health, the factors that contribute to it, and strategies for promoting a healthy heart.

Understanding Cardiovascular Health:
Cardiovascular health refers to the well-being of the heart and blood vessels. It encompasses the proper functioning of the heart, efficient circulation, and healthy blood pressure and cholesterol levels. A healthy cardiovascular system is crucial for delivering oxygen and nutrients to the body's tissues and organs.

Factors that Influence Cardiovascular Health:
a. Healthy Diet: Consuming a balanced diet rich in fruits, vegetables, whole grains, lean proteins, and healthy fats supports cardiovascular health. Limiting saturated and trans fats, sodium, and added sugars is important in preventing heart disease.
b. Regular Physical Activity: Engaging in regular aerobic exercise, such as brisk walking, jogging, cycling, or swimming, improves cardiovascular fitness, strengthens the heart, and helps maintain healthy blood pressure and cholesterol levels.
c. Maintaining a Healthy Weight: Maintaining a healthy weight reduces the strain on the heart and lowers the risk of cardiovascular disease. A combination of healthy eating and regular exercise can help achieve and maintain a healthy weight.
d. Tobacco Avoidance: Smoking damages blood vessels, raises blood pressure, and increases the risk of heart disease. Quitting smoking or avoiding tobacco use altogether is vital for cardiovascular health.
e. Limiting Alcohol Consumption: Excessive alcohol intake can lead to high blood pressure, irregular heart rhythms, and damage to the heart muscle. It is important to consume alcohol in moderation or avoid it altogether.

f. Managing Stress: Chronic stress can contribute to high blood pressure and an increased risk of heart disease. Implement stress management techniques such as exercise, relaxation techniques, and seeking social support to mitigate the negative effects of stress on cardiovascular health.
g. Regular Health Check-ups: Regular medical check-ups can help identify and manage risk factors for heart disease, such as high blood pressure, high cholesterol, and diabetes.
h. Adequate Sleep: Poor sleep quality and duration are associated with an increased risk of cardiovascular disease. Aim for 7-8 hours of quality sleep each night to support heart health.

Heart-Healthy Diet:
a. Eat a Variety of Fruits and Vegetables: These are rich in vitamins, minerals, fiber, and antioxidants that promote heart health.
b. Choose Whole Grains: Incorporate whole grains like brown rice, whole wheat bread, and oats into your diet for their fiber content and nutrients.
c. Include Lean Proteins: Opt for lean sources of protein such as skinless poultry, fish, legumes, and tofu. Limit the consumption of red meats and processed meats.
d. Healthy Fats: Include sources of healthy fats like avocados, nuts, seeds, olive oil, and fatty fish (salmon, mackerel) in your diet. These fats can help improve cholesterol levels and reduce inflammation.
e. Limit Sodium: Reduce your sodium intake by minimizing processed foods, restaurant meals, and adding less salt to your dishes.
f. Control Portion Sizes: Be mindful of portion sizes to avoid overeating and maintain a healthy weight.

Regular Physical Activity:
a. Aerobic Exercise: Engage in moderate-intensity aerobic activities for at least 150 minutes per week, or vigorous-intensity aerobic activities for 75 minutes per week. Choose activities you enjoy, such as walking, cycling, swimming, or dancing.
b. Strength Training: Incorporate strength training exercises at least twice a week to improve muscle strength and support cardiovascular health.
c. Active Lifestyle: Find opportunities to be physically active throughout the day, such as taking the stairs instead of the

elevator, walking or cycling instead of driving short distances, or participating in active hobbies or sports.

Seek Medical Advice:
If you have any concerns or pre-existing cardiovascular conditions, consult with your healthcare provider for personalized guidance and recommendations.

By adopting a heart-healthy lifestyle that includes a nutritious diet, regular physical activity, stress management, and avoidance of tobacco and excessive alcohol, you can support your cardiovascular health and reduce the risk of heart disease. Remember, small changes made consistently over time can have a significant impact on your heart health.

Obesity and Diabetes Prevention

Obesity and diabetes are significant health concerns worldwide. In this chapter, we will explore strategies for preventing and managing obesity and type 2 diabetes through lifestyle modifications, healthy eating habits, and regular physical activity.

Understanding Obesity and Type 2 Diabetes:
a. Obesity: Obesity is a condition characterized by excessive body fat accumulation, often resulting from an imbalance between energy intake and expenditure. It is associated with an increased risk of various health issues, including type 2 diabetes.
b. Type 2 Diabetes: Type 2 diabetes is a chronic metabolic disorder in which the body becomes resistant to insulin or does not produce enough insulin to regulate blood sugar levels. Obesity is a major risk factor for developing type 2 diabetes.

Promoting Healthy Eating Habits:
a. Balanced Diet: Adopt a balanced and nutritious eating plan that includes a variety of fruits, vegetables, whole grains, lean proteins, and healthy fats. Limit the consumption of processed and sugary foods.
b. Portion Control: Be mindful of portion sizes to avoid overeating. Use smaller plates and bowls, and listen to your body's hunger and fullness cues.
c. Reduce Added Sugars: Minimize the intake of foods and beverages high in added sugars, such as sodas, candies, pastries, and sweetened drinks.
d. Choose Healthy Fats: Include sources of healthy fats, such as avocados, nuts, seeds, and olive oil, while moderating saturated and trans fats.
e. Fiber-Rich Foods: Consume fiber-rich foods like whole grains, legumes, fruits, and vegetables. Fiber promotes satiety, aids in digestion, and helps regulate blood sugar levels.
f. Limit Processed Foods: Reduce the consumption of processed and ultra-processed foods that are often high in calories, unhealthy fats, sodium, and added sugars.
g. Mindful Eating: Practice mindful eating by slowing down, savoring each bite, and being aware of your body's hunger and fullness cues.

Regular Physical Activity:
a. Aerobic Exercise: Engage in moderate-intensity aerobic activities, such as brisk walking, jogging, cycling, or swimming, for at least 150 minutes per week. This helps burn calories, improve cardiovascular health, and manage weight.
b. Strength Training: Incorporate strength training exercises at least twice a week to build lean muscle mass, increase metabolism, and support weight management.
c. Active Lifestyle: Seek opportunities to be physically active throughout the day, such as taking the stairs, walking or cycling instead of driving short distances, and incorporating active hobbies or sports into your routine.

Weight Management:
a. Set Realistic Goals: Establish realistic and achievable weight loss goals. Aim for gradual, sustainable weight loss rather than rapid and temporary results.
b. Monitor Portion Sizes: Be mindful of portion sizes, and use tools such as measuring cups, food scales, or visual cues to ensure appropriate serving sizes.
c. Keep a Food Diary: Maintain a food diary to track your eating habits, identify patterns, and make adjustments accordingly.
d. Seek Professional Guidance: Consult a registered dietitian or healthcare professional for personalized advice and guidance on weight management strategies.

Lifestyle Modifications:
a. Stress Management: Develop healthy coping mechanisms for managing stress, such as practicing relaxation techniques, engaging in hobbies, or seeking support from friends, family, or professionals.
b. Adequate Sleep: Prioritize getting enough quality sleep, as insufficient sleep has been associated with weight gain and an increased risk of developing diabetes.
c. Tobacco and Alcohol Moderation: Avoid tobacco use, as it is linked to various health issues. Limit alcohol consumption and adhere to recommended guidelines.

Regular Health Check-ups:

a. Regular Health Monitoring: Schedule regular check-ups with your healthcare provider to monitor your weight, blood pressure, blood sugar levels, and overall health. Early detection and intervention can help prevent or manage obesity and diabetes.

Remember, prevention and management of obesity and diabetes require long-term commitment and lifestyle changes. By adopting a balanced diet, engaging in regular physical activity, maintaining a healthy weight, managing stress, and seeking professional guidance, you can reduce the risk of obesity and type 2 diabetes while improving your overall health and well-being.

Bone and Dental Health

Maintaining healthy bones and dental hygiene is essential for overall well-being. In this chapter, we will explore strategies for promoting strong bones, preventing bone-related conditions, and maintaining good dental health.

Promoting Bone Health:
a. Calcium-Rich Diet: Include calcium-rich foods in your diet, such as dairy products (milk, yogurt, cheese), leafy green vegetables (kale, spinach), fortified plant-based milk alternatives, and calcium-fortified foods.
b. Vitamin D: Ensure adequate vitamin D intake through sunlight exposure, fortified foods (cereals, orange juice), fatty fish (salmon, mackerel), and supplements if necessary. Vitamin D is essential for calcium absorption and bone health.
c. Magnesium and Vitamin K: Consume foods rich in magnesium (nuts, seeds, legumes, whole grains) and vitamin K (leafy green vegetables, broccoli, Brussels sprouts) to support bone health.
d. Weight-Bearing Exercise: Engage in weight-bearing exercises like walking, jogging, dancing, or strength training. These activities help strengthen bones and promote bone density.
e. Avoid Smoking and Limit Alcohol: Smoking and excessive alcohol consumption can negatively impact bone health. Quit smoking and limit alcohol intake to support optimal bone health.

Preventing Osteoporosis:
a. Maintain a Healthy Weight: Maintain a healthy weight through a balanced diet and regular physical activity. Excess weight can put strain on bones and increase the risk of osteoporosis.
b. Limit Caffeine and Soda: High consumption of caffeine and soda has been associated with reduced calcium absorption and potential negative effects on bone health. Consume these beverages in moderation.
c. Regular Bone Density Testing: If you are at higher risk for osteoporosis, such as postmenopausal women or individuals with certain medical conditions, discuss with your healthcare provider about regular bone density testing.

Dental Health and Hygiene:

a. Brush Twice a Day: Brush your teeth with fluoride toothpaste at least twice a day for two minutes each time. Use a soft-bristle toothbrush and replace it every three to four months.
b. Floss Daily: Floss your teeth daily to remove plaque and food particles from between the teeth and along the gumline.
c. Regular Dental Check-ups: Schedule regular dental check-ups and cleanings to maintain oral health and address any potential issues promptly.
d. Limit Sugary Foods and Drinks: Minimize the consumption of sugary foods and drinks, as they can contribute to tooth decay. Opt for healthier alternatives and practice good oral hygiene after consuming sugary items.
e. Drink Plenty of Water: Water helps rinse away food particles and stimulates saliva production, which helps prevent tooth decay. Choose fluoridated water when available.
f. Use Mouthwash: Consider using mouthwash as part of your oral hygiene routine to freshen breath and reduce bacteria in the mouth. Choose an alcohol-free mouthwash if you prefer.
g. Avoid Tobacco Use: Smoking and tobacco use can lead to gum disease, tooth loss, and oral cancers. Quitting smoking or avoiding tobacco products is essential for maintaining good dental health.

Protecting Teeth:
a. Wear Mouthguards: If you participate in contact sports or activities with a risk of dental injury, wear a mouthguard to protect your teeth and jaw.
b. Avoid Teeth Grinding: If you grind or clench your teeth, especially at night, discuss it with your dentist. They may recommend a mouthguard or other strategies to prevent tooth damage.
c. Be Mindful of Chewing Habits: Avoid chewing on hard objects like ice, pens, or hard candy, as it can lead to tooth fractures or damage.

Oral Health for Children:
a. Establish Healthy Habits Early: Teach children proper brushing and flossing techniques and encourage regular dental check-ups from a young age.
b. Limit Sugary Snacks and Drinks: Promote a healthy diet for children, limiting sugary snacks and drinks to prevent tooth decay.

c. Use Fluoride: Ensure children receive an adequate amount of fluoride for strong and healthy teeth. Discuss fluoride supplementation with a pediatric dentist or healthcare provider.

By following these strategies for promoting bone health, preventing osteoporosis, and maintaining good dental hygiene, you can support your overall well-being and enjoy strong bones and healthy teeth throughout your life. Remember to consult with healthcare professionals or dentists for personalized advice and guidance.

Boosting Immunity and Overall Well-Being

Maintaining a strong immune system and overall well-being is crucial for optimal health. In this chapter, we will explore strategies to boost immunity, support overall well-being, and promote a healthy lifestyle.

Balanced and Nutritious Diet:
a. Eat a Rainbow of Fruits and Vegetables: Include a variety of colorful fruits and vegetables in your diet to provide essential vitamins, minerals, and antioxidants that support immune function.
b. Protein-Rich Foods: Consume adequate amounts of lean proteins, such as poultry, fish, legumes, and tofu, to support immune system function.
c. Healthy Fats: Incorporate sources of healthy fats, such as avocados, nuts, seeds, and olive oil, which have anti-inflammatory properties and support immune health.
d. Probiotics and Fermented Foods: Include probiotics in your diet through sources like yogurt, kefir, sauerkraut, and kimchi. These help maintain a healthy gut microbiome, which plays a significant role in immune function.
e. Stay Hydrated: Drink plenty of water throughout the day to support overall health and ensure proper functioning of bodily systems, including the immune system.

Regular Physical Activity:
a. Engage in Aerobic Exercise: Participate in moderate-intensity aerobic activities like brisk walking, jogging, swimming, or cycling to enhance immune function and overall well-being.
b. Strength Training: Incorporate strength training exercises to build muscle strength, improve metabolism, and support overall fitness.
c. Maintain an Active Lifestyle: Find opportunities for physical activity throughout the day, such as taking regular walks, using stairs instead of elevators, or engaging in active hobbies.

Sufficient Sleep:
a. Prioritize Quality Sleep: Aim for 7-9 hours of quality sleep each night to allow your body to repair and rejuvenate. Lack of sleep can weaken the immune system and increase the risk of illnesses.

Stress Management:
a. Practice Stress-Reducing Techniques: Engage in stress-reducing activities such as meditation, deep breathing exercises, yoga, or mindfulness to manage stress levels and support immune health.
b. Find Healthy Outlets: Seek hobbies, social connections, and activities that bring joy and relaxation to help manage stress.

Hygiene and Illness Prevention:
a. Wash Hands Regularly: Proper hand hygiene is crucial in preventing the spread of infections. Wash your hands with soap and water for at least 20 seconds, especially before eating and after using the restroom.
b. Practice Respiratory Etiquette: Cover your mouth and nose with a tissue or your elbow when coughing or sneezing to prevent the spread of germs.
c. Stay Vaccinated: Stay up to date with recommended vaccinations to protect against common illnesses and promote overall health.

Healthy Relationships and Social Connections:
a. Nurture Relationships: Cultivate healthy and supportive relationships with family, friends, and communities, as they contribute to overall well-being and provide a sense of belonging.
b. Seek Support: Reach out to loved ones or professionals when needed for emotional support and guidance.

Avoid Harmful Substances:
a. Limit Alcohol Consumption: Drink alcohol in moderation or avoid it altogether, as excessive alcohol consumption can weaken the immune system and have negative effects on overall health.
b. Quit Smoking: If you smoke, take steps to quit. Smoking damages the immune system and increases the risk of various health conditions.

Regular Health Check-ups:
a. Routine Check-ups: Schedule regular check-ups with your healthcare provider for preventive care, screenings, and to address any health concerns.

Remember, maintaining a strong immune system and overall well-being is a lifelong commitment. By adopting a healthy lifestyle that includes a balanced diet, regular physical activity, sufficient sleep, stress management, good hygiene practices, and healthy relationships, you can boost your immune system, support your overall well-being, and reduce the risk of illness. Consult with healthcare professionals for personalized advice and recommendations.

The Role of Healthy Eating in Mental Health

Impact of Nutrition on Mood and Emotional Well-Being

Nutrition plays a crucial role in not only our physical health but also our mental and emotional well-being. In this chapter, we will explore the impact of nutrition on mood and emotional well-being and provide strategies for maintaining a healthy diet that supports positive mental health.

The Gut-Brain Connection:
a. Gut Microbiota: The gut microbiota, the community of microorganisms in our digestive system, influences our brain function and plays a role in regulating mood and emotions.
b. Neurotransmitters: The gut produces neurotransmitters, such as serotonin, dopamine, and gamma-aminobutyric acid (GABA), which are involved in regulating mood and emotional responses.

Nutrients and Mood:
a. Omega-3 Fatty Acids: Incorporate foods rich in omega-3 fatty acids, such as fatty fish (salmon, mackerel), walnuts, chia seeds, and flaxseeds. Omega-3s have been associated with reduced symptoms of depression and improved overall mood.
b. B Vitamins: Consume foods rich in B vitamins, including whole grains, legumes, leafy green vegetables, eggs, and lean meats. B vitamins, particularly folate and vitamin B12, are important for mood regulation and brain health.
c. Antioxidants: Eat a variety of fruits and vegetables rich in antioxidants, such as berries, dark leafy greens, and colorful vegetables. Antioxidants help reduce oxidative stress and inflammation, which can positively impact mood.
d. Tryptophan: Include foods high in tryptophan, an amino acid found in turkey, chicken, eggs, and dairy products. Tryptophan is a precursor to serotonin, a neurotransmitter associated with mood regulation.
e. Complex Carbohydrates: Choose complex carbohydrates like whole grains, legumes, and vegetables. They provide a steady release of energy and help support stable blood sugar levels, which can impact mood and energy levels.

Blood Sugar Balance:
a. Regular Meals: Eat balanced meals with a combination of carbohydrates, proteins, and healthy fats to maintain stable blood sugar levels throughout the day.
b. Avoid Refined Sugars: Minimize consumption of refined sugars and sugary snacks, as they can lead to blood sugar spikes followed by crashes, negatively affecting mood and energy levels.
c. Fiber-Rich Foods: Include fiber-rich foods like whole grains, fruits, and vegetables, as they help slow down the absorption of sugar and promote steady blood sugar levels.

Hydration:
a. Water Intake: Stay adequately hydrated by drinking enough water throughout the day. Dehydration can impact cognitive function, mood, and overall well-being.

Mindful Eating:
a. Pay Attention to Hunger and Fullness: Eat mindfully, paying attention to your body's hunger and fullness cues. Avoid emotional or stress-related eating, and instead choose nourishing foods that support your well-being.
b. Enjoy Your Meals: Take the time to savor and enjoy your meals, focusing on the flavors, textures, and sensations. This can help promote a positive relationship with food and enhance the satisfaction of eating.

Limiting Stimulants:
a. Caffeine: Be mindful of your caffeine intake and its effects on your mood and anxiety levels. Limit consumption or opt for decaffeinated versions if you are sensitive to its stimulating effects.
b. Alcohol: Moderate alcohol consumption, as excessive intake can negatively impact mood and mental health.

Seek Professional Support:
a. Consult with a Registered Dietitian: If you have specific concerns or questions about nutrition and mental health, consider seeking guidance from a registered dietitian who specializes in this area.
b. Mental Health Professionals: If you are experiencing significant mood disorders or emotional challenges, it is important to seek

support from mental health professionals who can provide appropriate evaluation and treatment.

Remember, nutrition is just one piece of the puzzle when it comes to mental and emotional well-being. It is important to seek a holistic approach that includes self-care, stress management, regular physical activity, and social support to support overall mental health.

Nutrition for Improved Focus and Memory

Proper nutrition plays a vital role in supporting cognitive function, focus, and memory. In this chapter, we will explore the impact of nutrition on brain health and provide strategies for incorporating a brain-healthy diet to improve focus and memory.

Brain-Boosting Nutrients:
a. Omega-3 Fatty Acids: Include sources of omega-3 fatty acids, such as fatty fish (salmon, mackerel), walnuts, chia seeds, and flaxseeds. Omega-3s support brain health, improve cognitive function, and enhance memory.
b. Antioxidants: Consume foods rich in antioxidants, including berries, dark leafy greens, and colorful fruits and vegetables. Antioxidants protect the brain from oxidative stress and inflammation, which can enhance cognitive function.
c. B Vitamins: Incorporate foods rich in B vitamins, such as whole grains, legumes, leafy green vegetables, eggs, and lean meats. B vitamins, particularly B6, B12, and folate, play a crucial role in brain health and cognitive function.
d. Choline: Consume foods high in choline, such as eggs, lean meats, fish, and cruciferous vegetables. Choline is important for memory and cognitive performance.
e. Vitamin E: Include sources of vitamin E, such as nuts, seeds, and vegetable oils. Vitamin E acts as an antioxidant and may help protect against cognitive decline.

Balanced Meals:
a. Complex Carbohydrates: Choose complex carbohydrates like whole grains, legumes, and vegetables, which provide a steady release of energy to support focus and mental clarity.
b. Proteins: Include lean sources of protein, such as poultry, fish, legumes, and tofu, to provide amino acids necessary for neurotransmitter production and brain function.
c. Healthy Fats: Incorporate healthy fats from sources like avocados, nuts, seeds, and olive oil. These fats support brain health and aid in nutrient absorption.
d. Colorful Fruits and Vegetables: Consume a variety of colorful fruits and vegetables, as they are rich in vitamins, minerals, and antioxidants that support brain function.

Hydration:
a. Drink Plenty of Water: Staying hydrated is essential for optimal brain function. Aim to drink enough water throughout the day to support cognitive performance and maintain mental clarity.

Mindful Eating:
a. Eat Regularly: Avoid skipping meals, as it can lead to decreased energy levels and impaired cognitive function. Fuel your body and brain with regular, balanced meals and snacks.
b. Minimize Distractions: Create a calm and focused eating environment by minimizing distractions such as screens or multitasking. Pay attention to your meal, savor the flavors, and engage your senses.

Limit Added Sugars and Processed Foods:
a. Reduce Added Sugars: Minimize consumption of foods and beverages high in added sugars, as they can lead to energy crashes and difficulty focusing.
b. Limit Processed Foods: Minimize intake of processed foods, which often lack essential nutrients and can negatively impact brain function.

Cognitive Stimulation and Mental Exercise:
a. Brain Training: Engage in activities that challenge and stimulate your brain, such as puzzles, reading, learning a new skill, or playing strategic games. These activities can help improve focus, memory, and cognitive abilities.
b. Physical Activity: Regular physical activity supports brain health and cognitive function by increasing blood flow and promoting the growth of new neurons.

Adequate Sleep:
a. Prioritize Quality Sleep: Aim for 7-9 hours of quality sleep each night to support memory consolidation and cognitive performance.

Manage Stress:
a. Stress Reduction Techniques: Practice stress management techniques such as deep breathing, meditation, yoga, or engaging

in activities that promote relaxation. Chronic stress can impair focus and memory.

Remember, nutrition is just one aspect of supporting focus and memory. It is important to maintain a balanced lifestyle that includes regular exercise, quality sleep, cognitive stimulation, and stress management techniques. By incorporating brain-healthy foods and lifestyle habits, you can optimize your cognitive function, enhance focus, and support long-term memory.

Wholesome Snacks and Desserts

Finding wholesome and nutritious snacks and desserts is essential for maintaining a balanced diet and satisfying your cravings. In this chapter, we will explore ideas for wholesome snacks and desserts that are delicious, satisfying, and support your overall well-being.

Wholesome Snack Ideas:
a. Fresh Fruits: Enjoy a variety of fresh fruits like apples, bananas, berries, oranges, or sliced melons. They provide natural sweetness, fiber, and essential vitamins.
b. Greek Yogurt: Opt for Greek yogurt, which is high in protein and calcium. Top it with fresh fruits, nuts, or a drizzle of honey for added flavor.
c. Nut Butter and Whole Grain Crackers: Spread natural nut butter (such as almond or peanut butter) on whole grain crackers for a satisfying and nutritious snack.
d. Veggie Sticks with Hummus: Snack on crisp vegetable sticks like carrots, cucumbers, and bell peppers, paired with hummus for a flavorful and fiber-rich option.
e. Homemade Trail Mix: Create your own trail mix by combining a variety of nuts, seeds, dried fruits, and dark chocolate chips for a balanced and energizing snack.
f. Hard-Boiled Eggs: Prepare a batch of hard-boiled eggs for a protein-rich and convenient snack. Sprinkle them with a pinch of salt or paprika for extra flavor.
g. Roasted Chickpeas: Toss chickpeas with olive oil and seasonings, then roast them until crispy for a savory and fiber-packed snack.
h. Homemade Energy Balls: Make energy balls using a combination of dates, nuts, seeds, and a touch of natural sweeteners like honey or maple syrup. They provide a satisfying blend of nutrients and can be customized with various flavors.
i. Popcorn: Opt for air-popped popcorn, seasoned with herbs, spices, or nutritional yeast for a light and whole-grain snack.
j. Cottage Cheese with Berries: Enjoy a serving of cottage cheese with a handful of fresh berries for a protein-rich snack that satisfies both sweet and savory cravings.

Wholesome Dessert Ideas:

a. Fruit Parfait: Layer Greek yogurt, mixed berries, and a sprinkle of granola or nuts for a refreshing and nutritious dessert.
b. Baked Fruit: Bake sliced apples or pears with a sprinkle of cinnamon and a drizzle of honey for a warm and comforting dessert.
c. Chia Seed Pudding: Prepare chia seed pudding using your choice of milk, chia seeds, and natural sweeteners like maple syrup or mashed fruits. Let it set in the refrigerator for a creamy and satisfying dessert.
d. Frozen Yogurt Bark: Spread Greek yogurt onto a baking sheet, and top it with chopped fruits, nuts, or dark chocolate. Freeze until solid, then break it into pieces for a refreshing and customizable dessert.
e. Dark Chocolate-Dipped Fruit: Dip fresh fruit slices (such as strawberries, bananas, or orange segments) into melted dark chocolate for a decadent and antioxidant-rich treat.
f. Homemade Fruit Sorbet: Blend frozen fruits like mangoes, berries, or pineapple with a splash of fruit juice or coconut water for a naturally sweet and refreshing sorbet.
g. Baked Oatmeal Cups: Make individual-sized baked oatmeal cups using oats, mashed bananas, and your choice of mix-ins like nuts, berries, or chocolate chips. They make for a wholesome and portable dessert.
h. Yogurt Parfait Popsicles: Layer Greek yogurt, fruit puree, and granola in popsicle molds, then freeze for a delightful and nutritious frozen treat.
i. Banana Nice Cream: Blend frozen bananas until creamy and smooth, and customize it with additions like cocoa powder, peanut butter, or frozen berries for a guilt-free and dairy-free ice cream alternative.
j. Homemade Fruit Crumble: Combine sliced fruits with a whole grain and nut crumble topping, then bake until golden and bubbly for a comforting and healthier dessert option.

Remember, moderation is key when enjoying snacks and desserts, even if they are wholesome and nutritious. These ideas provide healthier alternatives to traditional snacks and desserts, but it's still important to be mindful of portion sizes and listen to your body's hunger and fullness cues. Enjoy these wholesome treats as part of a balanced diet and lifestyle.

The Basics of Healthy Eating: A Beginner's Guide.

Practical Tips and Recommendations

Meal Planning and Menu Creation

Weekly Meal Planning

Weekly meal planning is an effective strategy for ensuring a well-balanced and nourishing diet while saving time and reducing stress. In this chapter, we will explore the benefits of meal planning and provide practical tips for successful weekly meal planning.

Benefits of Weekly Meal Planning:
a. Time and Effort Savings: Planning meals ahead of time saves you from daily decision-making and reduces time spent on grocery shopping and meal preparation.
b. Healthier Choices: Meal planning allows you to incorporate a variety of nutritious foods, ensuring a well-balanced diet and reducing reliance on processed or unhealthy options.
c. Cost Savings: Planning meals helps you make a shopping list and avoid impulse purchases, minimizing food waste and saving money.
d. Reduced Stress: Knowing what to cook in advance reduces mealtime stress and allows for a smoother cooking process.
e. Variety and Creativity: Meal planning enables you to introduce new recipes, try different cuisines, and experiment with diverse ingredients.

Meal Planning Steps:
a. Assess Your Schedule: Consider your schedule for the week, including work, family commitments, and social events. This will help you determine the number of meals to plan and if you need to account for leftovers or meals on-the-go.
b. Set Goals and Consider Nutritional Needs: Identify your dietary goals, whether it's consuming more vegetables, reducing processed foods, or meeting specific nutritional requirements.
c. Choose Recipes: Select a variety of recipes that align with your goals and preferences. Consider incorporating a mix of familiar favorites and new recipes to keep meals interesting.
d. Make a Grocery List: Based on the chosen recipes, create a comprehensive grocery list. Check your pantry and fridge for items you already have and prioritize fresh produce and perishable items.

e. Grocery Shopping: Allocate time for grocery shopping and try to stick to your list. Shopping once a week ensures you have all the necessary ingredients on hand.

f. Meal Preparation: Set aside time for meal preparation, such as chopping vegetables, marinating proteins, or pre-cooking certain components. This can save time during busy weekdays.

g. Storage and Labeling: Properly store prepped ingredients or meals in airtight containers, and label them with the recipe name and date to maintain freshness and organization.

h. Adaptability and Flexibility: Remain flexible with your meal plan, as unexpected changes may occur. Have backup options or leftovers available for those days when plans change.

Tips for Successful Weekly Meal Planning:

a. Theme Nights: Assign themes to different days of the week, such as Meatless Monday, Taco Tuesday, or Stir-Fry Friday. This helps provide structure and inspiration for meal choices.

b. Batch Cooking: Prepare larger portions of certain recipes that can be enjoyed as leftovers or frozen for future meals. This is particularly useful for soups, stews, and casseroles.

c. Plan for Convenience: Consider quick and easy meals for busy days, such as sheet pan dinners, one-pot meals, or slow cooker recipes that require minimal effort.

d. Utilize Seasonal Produce: Incorporate seasonal fruits and vegetables into your meal plan for optimal flavor, variety, and cost-effectiveness.

e. Prep Ingredients Ahead: Wash and chop vegetables, cook grains, or marinate proteins in advance to streamline meal preparation during the week.

f. Keep a Recipe Collection: Maintain a collection of favorite recipes or meal ideas for future reference. This can save time when planning meals and provide inspiration.

Mindful Portion Control:

a. Be mindful of portion sizes to ensure a balanced and appropriate calorie intake.

b. Consider using meal prep containers or portion control tools to maintain consistent serving sizes.

c. Listen to your body's hunger and fullness cues and adjust portion sizes accordingly.

Remember, weekly meal planning is a flexible tool, and it's important to adapt it to your individual needs and preferences. Experiment with different recipes, flavors, and cooking methods to keep your meals exciting and enjoyable. With consistent practice, meal planning will become a valuable habit that promotes a healthier lifestyle and reduces mealtime stress.

The Basics of Healthy Eating: A Beginner's Guide.

Grocery Shopping and Selecting Quality Ingredients

Effective grocery shopping is essential for obtaining fresh, nutritious ingredients and setting the foundation for healthy and delicious meals. In this chapter, we will explore strategies for grocery shopping and selecting high-quality ingredients to support your overall well-being.

Make a Shopping List:
a. Plan Ahead: Before heading to the grocery store, create a shopping list based on your meal plan and the ingredients you need. This helps you stay organized and prevents impulse purchases.
b. Prioritize Nutrient-Dense Foods: Include a variety of fruits, vegetables, whole grains, lean proteins, and healthy fats on your list to ensure a well-balanced and nutritious diet.
c. Check Pantry and Fridge: Take inventory of what you already have at home to avoid buying duplicates and reduce food waste.

Choose Fresh Produce:
a. Seasonal and Local: Opt for seasonal and locally sourced produce whenever possible. They are often fresher, more flavorful, and support sustainable agriculture.
b. Visual Assessment: Examine fruits and vegetables for signs of freshness, such as vibrant colors, firmness, and absence of bruises or blemishes. Avoid produce that appears wilted or overripe.
c. Organic Options: Consider organic produce, especially for items on the Environmental Working Group's "Dirty Dozen" list, which identifies fruits and vegetables with higher pesticide residues. However, prioritize consuming a variety of fruits and vegetables, regardless of organic or conventional status, as the health benefits outweigh potential pesticide exposure risks.

Select Quality Proteins:
a. Freshness and Appearance: Choose fresh cuts of meat, poultry, and seafood. They should have a pleasant smell, vibrant color, and appear moist, without any discoloration or strong odors.
b. Source and Animal Welfare: Opt for ethically sourced and sustainably raised proteins whenever possible. Look for

certifications like "organic," "grass-fed," or "wild-caught" to ensure higher quality and environmental sustainability.

Whole Grains and Legumes:
a. Read Labels: When purchasing packaged whole grains or legumes, read the ingredient list to ensure minimal processing and no added sugars or preservatives. Look for products with shorter ingredient lists and recognizable, whole food ingredients.
b. Bulk Section: Consider buying whole grains and legumes from the bulk section of the grocery store, as it allows you to choose quantities and reduces packaging waste.

Dairy and Plant-Based Alternatives:
a. Quality Dairy Products: Select dairy products that are fresh, preferably from local sources. Look for options with minimal additives or artificial ingredients.
b. Plant-Based Alternatives: When choosing plant-based alternatives, read ingredient labels to ensure they are made from whole foods and free from excessive additives or sweeteners.

Canned and Packaged Goods:
a. Read Labels: When purchasing canned or packaged goods, read ingredient labels to avoid high levels of added sugars, unhealthy fats, and excessive sodium. Look for options with recognizable, whole food ingredients and minimal additives.
b. Choose Low Sodium Options: Opt for low sodium or no salt added versions of canned goods, or rinse canned beans and vegetables to reduce sodium content.

Frozen Foods:
a. Nutrient Retention: Frozen fruits and vegetables can be just as nutritious as fresh ones, as they are often frozen at their peak ripeness. Look for options with no added sugars or sauces.
b. Check Packaging: Ensure that frozen foods are properly sealed and undamaged to maintain quality and prevent freezer burn.

Mindful Shopping:
a. Stick to the Perimeter: The perimeter of the grocery store typically houses fresh produce, meats, dairy, and whole foods. Focus on these areas to prioritize nutrient-dense options.

b. Minimize Processed Foods: Limit purchases of highly processed foods, such as sugary snacks, packaged desserts, and processed meats. They tend to be high in unhealthy fats, added sugars, and artificial ingredients.

c. Shop When Less Crowded: Choose less busy times for grocery shopping to have more time and space for careful ingredient selection.

Sustainable Choices:
a. Consider Environmental Impact: Opt for sustainably sourced seafood, fair-trade products, and products with minimal packaging to support environmentally friendly practices.

b. Bring Your Own Bags: Bring reusable shopping bags to reduce plastic waste.

Storage and Handling:
a. Proper Storage: Follow proper storage guidelines for different ingredients to maintain freshness and prevent spoilage. Store perishables in appropriate conditions, such as refrigeration or a cool, dry pantry.

b. FIFO (First In, First Out): Practice the FIFO method by using older ingredients before newer ones to prevent food waste.

Remember, grocery shopping is an opportunity to make conscious choices about the foods you bring into your home. By selecting fresh, high-quality ingredients and minimizing the purchase of processed and unhealthy options, you can support your overall well-being and create nutritious and delicious meals.

Food Preparation and Storage

Proper food preparation and storage practices are essential for maintaining food safety, preserving freshness, and maximizing the nutritional value of your ingredients. In this chapter, we will explore guidelines for safe and effective food preparation and storage.

Food Preparation:
a. Clean Hands and Surfaces: Wash your hands thoroughly with soap and water before handling food. Clean and sanitize kitchen surfaces, cutting boards, and utensils to prevent cross-contamination.
b. Separate Raw and Cooked Foods: Use separate cutting boards and utensils for raw meats and produce to prevent the spread of harmful bacteria.
c. Proper Thawing: Thaw frozen foods safely in the refrigerator, under cold running water, or in the microwave, following recommended guidelines. Avoid thawing at room temperature to minimize the risk of bacterial growth.
d. Safe Cooking Temperatures: Cook foods, especially meats, to their recommended internal temperatures to ensure they are safe to eat. Use a food thermometer to accurately measure the temperature.
e. Reheating: Reheat leftovers to a safe internal temperature of at least 165°F (74°C) to eliminate any potential bacteria.

Storage Guidelines:
a. Refrigeration: Store perishable foods, such as meat, poultry, dairy products, and prepared meals, in the refrigerator at or below 40°F (4°C) to slow down bacterial growth.
b. Freezing: Use the freezer to preserve food for longer periods. Package foods in airtight, freezer-safe containers or bags to maintain quality and prevent freezer burn.
c. Labeling: Label containers with the date and contents to track freshness and ensure timely use.
d. First In, First Out (FIFO): Practice FIFO by using older ingredients and leftovers before newer ones to minimize food waste.
e. Raw and Cooked Separation: Store raw meats separately from ready-to-eat foods to prevent cross-contamination.

f. Proper Packaging: Use appropriate storage containers to prevent air exposure and maintain the quality and flavor of foods.
g. Utilize Storage Solutions: Utilize organization tools such as clear containers, stackable bins, and shelf dividers to optimize space and keep track of stored items.

Fresh Produce:
a. Washing: Rinse fresh fruits and vegetables under running water before consuming or cooking to remove dirt, bacteria, and pesticide residues. Use a scrub brush for firmer produce.
b. Storage: Store produce appropriately based on their specific needs. Some items, like berries and lettuce, may require refrigeration, while others are best kept at room temperature.
c. Ethylene Sensitivity: Be aware of ethylene-sensitive produce (e.g., apples, bananas) that release the gas ethylene, which can accelerate ripening and spoilage in other fruits and vegetables. Store them separately or utilize ethylene-absorbing products.

Leftovers:
a. Prompt Refrigeration: Refrigerate leftovers promptly, within two hours of cooking, to prevent the growth of harmful bacteria.
b. Portion and Package: Divide large leftovers into smaller portions before refrigerating or freezing for easier and quicker reheating.
c. Safe Reheating: Reheat leftovers to a safe internal temperature to eliminate any potential bacteria. Stir or rotate the food during reheating for even heating.

Meal Prepping:
a. Batch Cooking: Prepare larger quantities of meals or components, such as grains, proteins, or roasted vegetables, to use throughout the week for quick and convenient meal assembly.
b. Portion Control: Use portioned containers or meal prep containers to ensure proper serving sizes and facilitate easy grab-and-go meals.
c. Refrigeration and Freezing: Store prepped meals and ingredients in airtight containers in the refrigerator for short-term use or freeze for longer-term storage.
d. Assembly and Seasoning: When prepping meals in advance, keep wet and dry ingredients separate until ready to consume to maintain texture and prevent sogginess.

Minimizing Food Waste:
a. Smart Shopping: Plan meals and create a shopping list to purchase only what you need. Avoid overbuying perishable items that may go to waste.
b. Repurposing Leftovers: Get creative with leftover ingredients or meals by transforming them into new dishes or incorporating them into soups, stews, or stir-fries.
c. Composting: Consider composting fruit and vegetable scraps to reduce food waste and create nutrient-rich soil for gardening.

By following proper food preparation and storage practices, you can ensure food safety, maintain freshness, and make the most of your ingredients. These practices contribute to healthier meals, reduced food waste, and overall kitchen efficiency.

Various Dietary Approaches

Vegetarianism and Veganism

Vegetarianism and veganism are dietary choices that exclude or limit the consumption of animal products. In this chapter, we will explore the principles, benefits, and considerations of vegetarianism and veganism.

Understanding Vegetarianism and Veganism:
a. Vegetarianism: Vegetarian diets eliminate meat, poultry, and seafood. However, there are variations within vegetarianism:

Lacto-vegetarian: Excludes meat, poultry, seafood, and eggs but includes dairy products.
Ovo-vegetarian: Excludes meat, poultry, seafood, and dairy products but includes eggs.
Lacto-ovo-vegetarian: Excludes meat, poultry, seafood but includes both dairy products and eggs.
b. Veganism: Vegan diets exclude all animal-derived products, including meat, poultry, seafood, eggs, dairy, and honey. Vegans also avoid using animal products in non-food items, such as clothing or cosmetics.
Health Benefits of Vegetarianism and Veganism:
a. Nutrient-Rich Diets: Well-planned vegetarian and vegan diets can be rich in fruits, vegetables, whole grains, legumes, nuts, and seeds, providing a wide range of essential nutrients.
b. Lower Risk of Chronic Diseases: Vegetarian and vegan diets have been associated with a reduced risk of heart disease, high blood pressure, type 2 diabetes, and certain cancers.
c. Increased Fiber Intake: Plant-based diets are generally high in fiber, which supports digestive health, promotes satiety, and helps regulate blood sugar levels.
d. Lower Environmental Impact: Plant-based diets tend to have a lower carbon footprint, require less water and land resources, and contribute to the preservation of biodiversity.

Key Nutrients to Consider:
a. Protein: Plant-based sources of protein include legumes (beans, lentils, chickpeas), tofu, tempeh, seitan, quinoa, nuts, and seeds.

Combining different protein sources throughout the day ensures adequate intake of essential amino acids.
b. Iron: Plant-based iron sources include legumes, tofu, spinach, kale, quinoa, fortified cereals, and nuts. Consuming iron-rich foods with a source of vitamin C, such as citrus fruits or bell peppers, enhances iron absorption.
c. Calcium: Plant-based calcium sources include fortified plant milks, calcium-set tofu, leafy greens (kale, collard greens), almonds, sesame seeds, and fortified orange juice.
d. Vitamin B12: Vitamin B12 is primarily found in animal products. Vegans should consider supplementation or consume fortified foods, such as plant-based milks or breakfast cereals, to ensure adequate intake.
e. Omega-3 Fatty Acids: Vegans can obtain omega-3 fatty acids from plant sources like flaxseeds, chia seeds, walnuts, and hemp seeds. Consider adding an algae-based omega-3 supplement to ensure adequate intake of DHA and EPA.

Practical Tips for Vegetarianism and Veganism:
a. Meal Planning: Plan meals in advance to ensure a well-balanced and varied diet that meets nutritional needs. Include a variety of fruits, vegetables, whole grains, legumes, nuts, and seeds.
b. Experiment with New Foods: Explore the wide range of plant-based foods and recipes available. Try new fruits, vegetables, grains, and plant-based proteins to discover new flavors and textures.
c. Recipe Modifications: Adapt traditional recipes by substituting animal products with plant-based alternatives. For example, use tofu or tempeh instead of meat in stir-fries or incorporate plant-based milks in baking.
d. Read Labels: Check food labels for hidden animal-derived ingredients, such as gelatin, whey, or casein. Familiarize yourself with common non-vegan additives and be cautious of processed foods that may contain animal products.
e. Seek Support and Information: Join vegetarian or vegan communities, attend cooking classes, or consult with registered dietitians or nutritionists who specialize in plant-based diets for guidance and support.

Considerations for Balanced Nutrition:

a. Variety and Balance: Include a wide range of plant-based foods to ensure a diverse nutrient intake. Aim for a balance of grains, legumes, fruits, vegetables, nuts, and seeds.
b. Protein Combinations: Combine different plant-based protein sources throughout the day to obtain a complete range of essential amino acids.
c. Fortified Foods and Supplements: Consider fortified plant-based milks, cereals, and nutritional yeast to supplement nutrients like calcium, vitamin D, and vitamin B12. Discuss your specific needs with a healthcare professional.
d. Monitoring Nutrient Levels: Periodically assess nutrient levels through blood tests to ensure adequate intake of essential nutrients, especially vitamin B12, iron, and vitamin D.

Remember, individual dietary needs may vary, and it's important to tailor your vegetarian or vegan diet to meet your specific nutritional requirements. Seek guidance from healthcare professionals or registered dietitians who specialize in plant-based nutrition to ensure a well-balanced and nourishing approach to vegetarianism or veganism.

Paleo and Ketogenic Diets

The Paleo and Ketogenic diets are two popular dietary approaches that have gained attention for their potential health benefits. In this chapter, we will explore the principles, benefits, and considerations of the Paleo and Ketogenic diets.

The Paleo Diet:
a. Principles: The Paleo diet, also known as the Paleolithic or Caveman diet, is based on the premise of eating foods that were available to our ancestors during the Paleolithic era. It emphasizes whole, unprocessed foods and eliminates grains, legumes, dairy products, processed foods, and added sugars.
b. Food Focus: The Paleo diet emphasizes lean meats, fish, fruits, vegetables, nuts, seeds, and healthy fats. It encourages the consumption of high-quality, grass-fed or wild-caught meats, and organic, locally sourced produce.
c. Potential Benefits: Advocates of the Paleo diet claim benefits such as improved blood sugar control, weight management, increased consumption of nutrient-dense foods, and reduced intake of processed and inflammatory foods.
d. Considerations: The Paleo diet restricts certain food groups, such as grains and legumes, which may limit the intake of important nutrients like fiber and certain vitamins. It is important to ensure adequate nutrient intake and variety within the allowed food choices.

The Ketogenic Diet:
a. Principles: The Ketogenic diet, or Keto diet, is a low-carbohydrate, high-fat diet that aims to shift the body into a metabolic state called ketosis. It involves drastically reducing carbohydrate intake and increasing fat consumption, which prompts the body to burn fat for fuel.
b. Macronutrient Ratios: The typical Keto diet consists of high fat (70-75% of calories), moderate protein (20-25% of calories), and very low carbohydrates (5-10% of calories).
c. Food Focus: The Keto diet encourages the consumption of healthy fats, such as avocados, olive oil, nuts, seeds, and coconut oil, along with moderate protein from sources like meat, poultry,

fish, and tofu. It restricts or limits carbohydrates, including grains, starchy vegetables, fruits, and added sugars.

d. Potential Benefits: The Keto diet has been associated with weight loss, improved insulin sensitivity, reduced inflammation, and increased mental clarity and energy. It may also be used as a therapeutic approach for certain medical conditions, such as epilepsy or metabolic disorders.

e. Considerations: The Keto diet requires careful planning to ensure adequate nutrient intake and prevent potential nutrient deficiencies. It may not be suitable for everyone, and individuals with certain medical conditions or on specific medications should consult with healthcare professionals before adopting this diet.

General Considerations:

a. Individual Variations: Dietary needs and responses to different diets can vary among individuals. It is important to listen to your body and tailor the diet to your specific needs, considering factors such as age, activity level, health status, and personal preferences.

b. Nutrient Adequacy: Both the Paleo and Ketogenic diets may require careful attention to ensure sufficient intake of essential nutrients, such as fiber, vitamins, and minerals. Incorporating a wide variety of nutrient-dense foods and, if necessary, considering supplementation can help meet nutritional needs.

c. Long-Term Sustainability: Consider the long-term sustainability and practicality of the chosen diet. Lifestyle factors, cultural considerations, and individual preferences should be taken into account to ensure adherence and overall well-being.

d. Individual Goals: The suitability of the Paleo or Ketogenic diets depends on individual goals and health conditions. Consulting with a registered dietitian or healthcare professional can provide personalized guidance based on specific needs and goals.

Remember, each person is unique, and there is no one-size-fits-all approach to nutrition. It is important to make informed decisions, listen to your body, and consider professional guidance when adopting any dietary approach. A well-balanced, varied diet that includes a wide range of whole, unprocessed foods is generally recommended for long-term health and well-being.

Gluten and Lactose Intolerance

Gluten and lactose intolerance are two common food intolerances that can cause discomfort and digestive issues in individuals. In this chapter, we will explore the characteristics, symptoms, management, and dietary considerations for gluten and lactose intolerance.

Gluten Intolerance:
a. Understanding Gluten: Gluten is a protein found in wheat, barley, rye, and some other grains. In individuals with gluten intolerance, the immune system reacts to gluten, leading to digestive symptoms and inflammation.
b. Celiac Disease: Celiac disease is an autoimmune condition where the ingestion of gluten triggers an immune response, causing damage to the lining of the small intestine. It requires strict avoidance of gluten-containing foods.
c. Non-Celiac Gluten Sensitivity: Some individuals may experience symptoms similar to celiac disease but without the characteristic intestinal damage. This is known as non-celiac gluten sensitivity, and it requires avoiding gluten to alleviate symptoms.
d. Symptoms: Symptoms of gluten intolerance can vary but commonly include bloating, abdominal pain, diarrhea or constipation, fatigue, and headaches.
e. Gluten-Free Diet: The primary treatment for gluten intolerance is following a gluten-free diet. This involves avoiding foods and ingredients that contain gluten, such as wheat, barley, rye, and processed foods made with these grains. Gluten-free alternatives, such as rice, quinoa, corn, and gluten-free grains, can be consumed instead.

Lactose Intolerance:
a. Understanding Lactose: Lactose is the natural sugar found in milk and dairy products. Lactose intolerance occurs when the body lacks the enzyme lactase, which is needed to break down lactose into simpler forms that can be digested.
b. Symptoms: Lactose intolerance symptoms typically include bloating, gas, abdominal pain, diarrhea, and sometimes nausea after consuming lactose-containing foods or drinks.

c. Management: The management of lactose intolerance involves reducing or eliminating lactose from the diet. Many individuals with lactose intolerance can tolerate small amounts of lactose, while others may need to avoid it completely.
d. Lactose-Free Alternatives: There are various lactose-free or lactose-reduced dairy products available, including lactose-free milk, yogurt, and cheese. Additionally, there are plant-based milk alternatives, such as almond milk, soy milk, or oat milk, that do not contain lactose.
e. Calcium Considerations: Since dairy products are a primary source of calcium, it is important for individuals with lactose intolerance to ensure sufficient calcium intake through other sources, such as fortified plant-based milk, leafy greens, almonds, and calcium supplements if necessary.

Dietary Considerations:
a. Reading Labels: When managing gluten or lactose intolerance, it is crucial to read food labels carefully to identify hidden sources of gluten or lactose. Look for terms like "wheat," "barley," "rye," "malt," or "milk" on ingredient lists.
b. Cross-Contamination: Individuals with gluten or lactose intolerance should be cautious about cross-contamination. It is important to ensure that gluten-free or lactose-free foods are not prepared or served alongside gluten-containing or lactose-containing foods.
c. Gluten-Free and Lactose-Free Alternatives: Many gluten-free and lactose-free alternatives are available in grocery stores, including gluten-free bread, pasta, and baking mixes, as well as lactose-free dairy products and non-dairy alternatives.
d. Nutrient Adequacy: While managing gluten or lactose intolerance, it is important to ensure a well-balanced diet that provides essential nutrients. Consult with a registered dietitian or healthcare professional to ensure proper nutrient intake and consider supplementation if necessary.
e. Individual Sensitivities: It is worth noting that individuals may have different sensitivities and tolerances. Some individuals with lactose intolerance, for example, may be able to tolerate small amounts of lactose without symptoms. Pay attention to your body's response to different foods and make adjustments accordingly.

Remember, if you suspect you have gluten or lactose intolerance, it is recommended to consult with a healthcare professional for an accurate diagnosis. They can provide personalized advice, recommend appropriate tests if needed, and guide you in managing your specific food intolerances while maintaining a well-balanced and nutritious diet.

Handy Collection of Healthy Recipes

Nutritious Breakfast Options

Breakfast is often considered the most important meal of the day, providing you with the energy and nutrients needed to kick-start your morning. In this chapter, we will explore a variety of nutritious breakfast options that can help you start your day on a healthy note.

Whole Grain Cereal:
a. Choose whole grain cereals that are low in added sugars and high in fiber. Look for options like oatmeal, bran flakes, or whole grain granola.
b. Top your cereal with fresh fruits, such as berries, sliced bananas, or diced apples, to add natural sweetness and additional nutrients.
c. Opt for milk or plant-based alternatives, like almond milk or soy milk, to pour over your cereal.

Overnight Chia Pudding:
a. Mix chia seeds with your choice of milk or plant-based yogurt in a jar or container.
b. Add flavorings like vanilla extract, cinnamon, or cocoa powder, and sweeten with a natural sweetener like honey or maple syrup.
c. Let the mixture sit in the refrigerator overnight to allow the chia seeds to absorb the liquid and create a pudding-like consistency.
d. In the morning, top with fresh fruits, nuts, or shredded coconut for added texture and flavor.

Greek Yogurt Parfait:
a. Layer Greek yogurt with fresh fruits, such as berries, sliced peaches, or mango chunks, in a glass or bowl.
b. Sprinkle with a handful of granola or nuts for crunch and added nutrients.
c. Drizzle with a touch of honey or maple syrup for sweetness, if desired.

Veggie Omelette:
a. Beat eggs or egg whites in a bowl and season with salt, pepper, and herbs of your choice.

b. Heat a non-stick pan and add diced vegetables like bell peppers, spinach, mushrooms, and onions.
c. Pour the beaten eggs over the vegetables and cook until set, flipping once if desired.
d. Serve with a side of whole grain toast or a handful of mixed greens.

Whole Grain Toast with Avocado and Egg:
a. Toast a slice of whole grain bread until golden and crisp.
b. Mash half an avocado and spread it on the toast.
c. Top with a poached or scrambled egg and sprinkle with salt, pepper, and optional herbs or spices like chili flakes or paprika.

Smoothie Bowl:
a. Blend frozen fruits like berries, bananas, or mangoes with a liquid base like almond milk, coconut water, or yogurt until smooth and creamy.
b. Pour the smoothie into a bowl and top with a variety of toppings, such as sliced fruits, granola, chia seeds, coconut flakes, or nuts.

Whole Grain Pancakes or Waffles:
a. Make a batch of homemade whole grain pancakes or waffles using whole wheat flour, oats, or a combination of flours.
b. Serve with a dollop of Greek yogurt or a drizzle of nut butter for added protein.
c. Top with fresh fruits, a sprinkle of cinnamon, or a small amount of pure maple syrup.

Breakfast Burrito:
a. Fill a whole grain wrap or tortilla with scrambled eggs or tofu, sautéed vegetables, and a sprinkle of cheese or nutritional yeast.
b. Add optional toppings like salsa, avocado slices, or a dollop of Greek yogurt for added flavor.

Fruit and Nut Butter Wrap:
a. Spread nut butter like almond butter or peanut butter on a whole grain wrap or tortilla.
b. Place sliced fruits, such as apples, bananas, or berries, on top of the nut butter.

c. Sprinkle with a small amount of granola or crushed nuts, and roll it up into a wrap.

Quinoa Breakfast Bowl:
a. Cook quinoa according to package instructions and let it cool slightly.
b. Add your favorite mix-ins like chopped nuts, dried fruits, seeds, and a drizzle of honey or maple syrup.
c. You can also add spices like cinnamon or vanilla extract for extra flavor.

Remember, a nutritious breakfast should include a balance of complex carbohydrates, protein, healthy fats, and fiber. Customize these breakfast options based on your preferences and dietary needs, and aim to include a variety of fruits, vegetables, whole grains, and lean protein sources to start your day off on a nourishing note.

Healthy Lunches and Dinners

Lunch and dinner are key meals that provide opportunities to fuel your body with nutritious foods and enjoy flavorful, satisfying meals. In this chapter, we will explore a variety of healthy lunch and dinner ideas that incorporate a balance of essential nutrients.

Grilled Chicken Salad:
a. Grill or bake a skinless chicken breast and slice it into strips.
b. Toss mixed greens, cherry tomatoes, cucumber slices, and bell peppers together.
c. Top the salad with the grilled chicken and add a sprinkle of feta cheese or sliced almonds for added flavor and texture.
d. Drizzle with a light vinaigrette dressing or a squeeze of lemon juice.

Quinoa and Vegetable Stir-Fry:
a. Cook quinoa according to package instructions.
b. In a pan, sauté an assortment of colorful vegetables such as broccoli, bell peppers, carrots, and snap peas with garlic and ginger.
c. Add cooked quinoa to the pan and stir-fry for a few minutes.
d. Season with low-sodium soy sauce or tamari, and sprinkle with sesame seeds or chopped green onions.

Lentil and Vegetable Soup:
a. In a pot, sauté onions, garlic, and your choice of vegetables like carrots, celery, and zucchini.
b. Add rinsed lentils and vegetable broth, and simmer until the lentils are tender.
c. Season with herbs and spices like thyme, cumin, and paprika, and add a handful of spinach or kale for added nutrients.
d. Serve the soup with a side of whole grain bread or a green salad.

Baked Salmon with Roasted Vegetables:
a. Season a salmon fillet with herbs, lemon juice, and a touch of olive oil.
b. Place the salmon on a baking sheet and surround it with a variety of vegetables like Brussels sprouts, asparagus, and cherry tomatoes.

c. Roast in the oven until the salmon is cooked through and the vegetables are tender and slightly caramelized.
d. Serve with a side of quinoa or brown rice for a complete meal.

Chickpea and Vegetable Curry:
a. Sauté onions, garlic, and your choice of vegetables like bell peppers, cauliflower, and sweet potatoes in a large pan.
b. Add chickpeas, diced tomatoes, and a blend of spices like curry powder, turmeric, cumin, and coriander.
c. Simmer until the vegetables are cooked and flavors have melded together.
d. Serve the curry over brown rice or quinoa, and garnish with fresh cilantro.

Veggie and Hummus Wrap:
a. Spread a whole grain wrap or tortilla with your favorite hummus.
b. Fill it with a variety of fresh vegetables like lettuce, sliced cucumbers, bell peppers, and shredded carrots.
c. Optional: Add some sliced avocado or crumbled feta cheese for added creaminess and flavor.
d. Roll up the wrap and slice it in half for a satisfying and portable lunch option.

Turkey or Tofu Lettuce Wraps:
a. Cook ground turkey or crumbled tofu with onions, garlic, and your choice of seasonings like ginger, soy sauce, and chili flakes.
b. Spoon the cooked mixture onto large lettuce leaves, such as romaine or butter lettuce.
c. Top with shredded carrots, sliced bell peppers, and a drizzle of hoisin sauce or peanut sauce.
d. Wrap the lettuce leaves around the filling and enjoy a light and flavorful meal.

Mediterranean Quinoa Salad:
a. Cook quinoa according to package instructions and let it cool.
b. Mix the quinoa with chopped cucumbers, cherry tomatoes, Kalamata olives, feta cheese, and fresh herbs like parsley and mint.
c. Drizzle with a lemon and olive oil dressing, and toss to combine.
d. Serve as a light and refreshing lunch or side dish with grilled chicken or fish.

Sweet Potato and Black Bean Tacos:
a. Roast sweet potato wedges in the oven until tender and slightly caramelized.
b. Mash black beans with spices like cumin, chili powder, and garlic powder.
c. Warm up corn tortillas and spread the mashed black beans on each tortilla.
d. Top with roasted sweet potatoes, sliced avocado, chopped tomatoes, and a sprinkle of cilantro.

Soba Noodle Stir-Fry:
a. Cook soba noodles according to package instructions and drain.
b. In a pan, stir-fry a mix of colorful vegetables like broccoli, snow peas, mushrooms, and bell peppers.
c. Add the cooked soba noodles to the pan and toss with a flavorful sauce made from low-sodium soy sauce, ginger, garlic, and a touch of honey or maple syrup.
d. Garnish with sesame seeds and chopped green onions before serving.

Remember, these lunch and dinner ideas are just a starting point. Feel free to customize them based on your dietary preferences, incorporate a variety of vegetables, lean proteins, whole grains, and healthy fats. Eating a balanced, nutrient-rich diet is important for overall health and well-being.

Wholesome Snacks and Desserts

Snacks and desserts can be enjoyed as part of a healthy diet when they are made with nutritious ingredients and consumed in moderation. In this chapter, we will explore a variety of wholesome snack and dessert options that provide both satisfaction and nourishment.

Wholesome Snacks:

Fresh Fruit:
a. Enjoy a piece of whole fruit, such as an apple, banana, orange, or a handful of berries.
b. Pair fruit with a source of protein, like a small handful of nuts or a dollop of nut butter, for added satiety.

Veggie Sticks with Hummus:
a. Slice fresh vegetables like carrot sticks, cucumber rounds, or bell pepper strips.
b. Dip the veggie sticks into a serving of homemade or store-bought hummus for a nutritious and satisfying snack.

Greek Yogurt Parfait:
a. Layer Greek yogurt with fresh fruits, such as berries or sliced peaches, in a small glass or bowl.
b. Sprinkle with a small handful of granola or chopped nuts for added crunch and texture.

Trail Mix:
a. Create your own trail mix by combining a variety of nuts, seeds, and dried fruits.
b. Add optional ingredients like dark chocolate chips or whole grain cereal for extra flavor and variety.

Hard-Boiled Eggs:
a. Hard-boil a few eggs and keep them in the fridge for a convenient and protein-rich snack.
b. Sprinkle with a pinch of salt, pepper, or your favorite seasoning for added flavor.

Rice Cakes with Toppings:
a. Top a plain rice cake with a spread of nut butter or avocado slices.
b. Sprinkle with a touch of cinnamon, chia seeds, or a drizzle of honey for a satisfying and crunchy snack.

Roasted Chickpeas:
a. Rinse and drain a can of chickpeas and pat them dry.
b. Toss the chickpeas with a bit of olive oil and your choice of spices, such as paprika, cumin, or garlic powder.
c. Roast them in the oven until crispy for a flavorful and protein-packed snack.

Wholesome Desserts:

Fruit Salad:
a. Combine a variety of chopped fruits, such as melons, grapes, pineapple, and kiwi, in a bowl.
b. Optional: Squeeze a bit of lime or lemon juice over the fruit to enhance the flavors.
c. Sprinkle with shredded coconut or a small handful of chopped nuts for added texture.

Yogurt and Berries:
a. Serve a portion of Greek yogurt or a dairy-free alternative in a bowl.
b. Top with a generous amount of fresh berries, such as strawberries, blueberries, or raspberries.
c. Drizzle with a small amount of honey or maple syrup if desired.

Dark Chocolate-Covered Fruit:
a. Melt a small amount of dark chocolate (70% cocoa or higher) using a double boiler or microwave.
b. Dip bite-sized pieces of fresh fruit, such as strawberries, banana slices, or orange segments, into the melted chocolate.
c. Place them on a parchment-lined tray and refrigerate until the chocolate sets.

Chia Seed Pudding:

a. Mix chia seeds with your choice of milk or plant-based yogurt in a jar or container.
b. Add flavorings like vanilla extract, cocoa powder, or cinnamon, and sweeten with a natural sweetener like honey or maple syrup.
c. Let the mixture sit in the refrigerator for a few hours or overnight until it thickens into a pudding-like consistency.
d. Top with fresh fruits, nuts, or a sprinkle of granola for added texture.

Baked Apples:
a. Core an apple and place it in a baking dish.
b. Fill the apple cavity with a mixture of oats, cinnamon, chopped nuts, and a small amount of honey or maple syrup.
c. Bake in the oven until the apple is tender and the filling is golden and fragrant.

Remember to enjoy snacks and desserts mindfully, savoring each bite and appreciating the flavors. Keep portion sizes in mind and incorporate these treats as part of a well-rounded and balanced diet.

Sustaining Healthy Eating in Everyday Life

Overcoming Challenges and Temptations

Dealing with Cravings and Overeating

Cravings and overeating can be challenging to manage, but with mindful strategies and a balanced approach, it is possible to regain control and develop healthier habits. In this chapter, we will explore various techniques to help deal with cravings and prevent overeating.

Understand Your Cravings:
a. Identify Triggers: Recognize the situations, emotions, or activities that tend to trigger your cravings. Is it stress, boredom, or certain social situations?
b. Explore the Underlying Causes: Cravings can be a result of physiological factors, such as nutrient deficiencies or hormonal changes, or psychological factors, such as emotional eating or habit formation.
c. Distinguish Hunger from Cravings: Learn to differentiate between true physical hunger and cravings. Ask yourself if you are truly hungry or if it is a desire for a specific food or taste.

Practice Mindful Eating:
a. Slow Down: Eat slowly and savor each bite. Pay attention to the taste, texture, and aroma of your food. This allows you to be more in tune with your body's satiety cues.
b. Listen to Your Body: Tune in to your body's signals of hunger and fullness. Eat until you feel satisfied, not overly full.
c. Eliminate Distractions: Avoid eating in front of screens or engaging in other activities. Focus on your meal or snack and enjoy the experience.

Plan Ahead:
a. Balanced Meals: Create balanced meals that include a variety of nutrients, including protein, healthy fats, fiber, and complex carbohydrates. This helps to provide satiety and reduce the likelihood of intense cravings.

b. Snack Options: Have wholesome snack options readily available, such as fresh fruits, cut vegetables, nuts, or Greek yogurt. These healthier choices can satisfy cravings and provide nourishment.
c. Meal Preparation: Plan and prepare your meals in advance, including snacks. This reduces the chances of reaching for unhealthy options when hunger strikes.

Choose Nutrient-Dense Foods:
a. Include Protein: Protein-rich foods, such as lean meats, poultry, fish, legumes, and tofu, can help promote satiety and reduce cravings.
b. Healthy Fats: Incorporate sources of healthy fats, such as avocados, nuts, seeds, and olive oil, into your meals. They provide a feeling of fullness and can help satisfy cravings.
c. Fiber-Rich Foods: Foods high in fiber, like whole grains, fruits, vegetables, and legumes, can help keep you feeling fuller for longer and reduce the likelihood of overeating.

Practice Portion Control:
a. Be Mindful of Portions: Be aware of portion sizes and practice portion control. Use smaller plates or bowls to help visually control portion sizes.
b. Slow Down: Take your time while eating, allowing your body to register fullness. Pause between bites and assess if you are still hungry before reaching for more.
c. Serve Pre-Portioned Meals and Snacks: Pre-portion meals and snacks to avoid mindless eating or overeating. This helps create a clear boundary for your intake.

Emotional Well-being:
a. Find Alternative Coping Mechanisms: If emotions trigger overeating or cravings, find alternative ways to manage them, such as engaging in physical activity, practicing deep breathing, journaling, or talking to a supportive friend or family member.
b. Stress Management: Implement stress management techniques, such as regular exercise, meditation, or hobbies that help reduce stress levels. This can prevent emotional eating and curb cravings.

Seek Support:

a. Accountability Buddy: Partner up with a friend or family member who shares similar health goals. Hold each other accountable and provide support during challenging times.
b. Professional Guidance: Consider consulting with a registered dietitian or a therapist who specializes in eating behaviors. They can provide personalized strategies and support to overcome cravings and overeating.

Practice Self-Compassion:
a. Avoid Guilt or Judgment: Be kind to yourself if you do give in to cravings or overeat. Remember that it is normal to have occasional indulgences, and one lapse does not define your overall eating habits.
b. Learn from Experiences: Reflect on the situations that led to overeating or intense cravings. Use these experiences as learning opportunities to make more mindful choices in the future.

Remember, it takes time and practice to develop healthier habits and manage cravings effectively. Be patient with yourself and celebrate small victories along the way. With consistency and self-awareness, you can regain control over your eating habits and foster a healthier relationship with food.

Mindful Eating and Mindful Food Choices

Mindful eating and making mindful food choices involve being present and aware of your eating experiences and making deliberate decisions about the foods you consume. By practicing mindfulness, you can develop a healthier relationship with food and make choices that support your overall well-being. In this chapter, we will explore the principles and techniques of mindful eating and making mindful food choices.

Principles of Mindful Eating:
a. Awareness: Pay attention to your physical sensations, emotions, and thoughts related to food. Notice hunger and fullness cues, as well as any cravings or emotional triggers.
b. Non-Judgment: Approach your eating experiences without judgment or criticism. Accept and embrace your feelings and choices, fostering a compassionate attitude towards yourself.
c. Slow Down: Eat slowly and savor each bite. Allow yourself to fully experience the flavors, textures, and aromas of your food.
d. Engage Your Senses: Use your senses of sight, smell, taste, and touch to fully experience your meals. Notice the colors, smells, and tastes of the foods you consume.
e. Listen to Your Body: Tune in to your body's hunger and fullness signals. Eat when you are physically hungry and stop eating when you feel comfortably satisfied.

Mindful Food Choices:
a. Conscious Awareness: Before choosing a food, pause and check in with yourself. Ask yourself if you are truly hungry or if you are craving a specific food for emotional reasons.
b. Nutrient Density: Consider the nutritional value of foods. Choose whole, unprocessed foods that are rich in nutrients, such as fruits, vegetables, whole grains, lean proteins, and healthy fats.
c. Balance and Moderation: Strive for a balanced approach to eating. Include a variety of food groups and practice moderation, avoiding extremes or restrictive behaviors.
d. Mindful Portions: Be mindful of portion sizes and avoid mindless eating. Serve yourself appropriate portions and listen to your body's signals of fullness.

e. Individual Preferences: Consider your personal preferences and values when making food choices. Choose foods that you enjoy and that align with your cultural or ethical beliefs.

Techniques for Mindful Eating:
a. Eating Rituals: Create rituals around your meals, such as setting a pleasant table, lighting a candle, or taking a few deep breaths before eating. These rituals can help you transition into a mindful eating mindset.
b. Mindful Mealtime: Create a calm and distraction-free environment during mealtime. Turn off electronic devices and focus solely on your food and the eating experience.
c. Chew Slowly and Thoroughly: Take the time to chew your food slowly and thoroughly. This aids in digestion, allows you to savor the flavors, and helps you feel more satisfied.
d. Engage Your Senses: Before taking a bite, observe the colors, textures, and smells of your food. As you eat, focus on the taste, texture, and sensations in your mouth.
e. Check in with Your Hunger and Fullness: Pause during your meal to assess your hunger and fullness levels. Take note of how satisfied you feel and adjust your eating accordingly.

Mindful Food Preparation:
a. Mindful Shopping: Approach grocery shopping with intention and awareness. Make a shopping list based on your meal plans and choose foods that align with your health goals.
b. Fresh and Whole Foods: Prioritize fresh and whole foods in your meal preparations. Cook from scratch whenever possible, using natural ingredients and minimizing the use of processed foods.
c. Appreciation for Ingredients: Take the time to appreciate the ingredients you use in your meals. Notice the colors, textures, and aromas of the foods as you prepare them.
d. Mindful Cooking: Engage in the process of cooking with presence and attention. Focus on each step, such as chopping vegetables or stirring a sauce, and enjoy the sensory experience.
e. Gratitude for Nourishment: Express gratitude for the nourishment that food provides. Cultivate a sense of appreciation for the effort and energy that went into producing and preparing your meal.

By practicing mindful eating and making mindful food choices, you can develop a healthier and more balanced approach to food. These practices encourage a deeper connection with your body and help you make decisions that support your overall well-being. Remember that mindful eating is a journey, and it takes time and practice to develop these habits. Embrace the process and be kind to yourself along the way.

The Basics of Healthy Eating: A Beginner's Guide.

Handling Social Situations and Events

Social situations and events often revolve around food, making it challenging to maintain healthy habits and make mindful choices. However, with some preparation and strategies in place, you can navigate these situations while still enjoying yourself and prioritizing your well-being. In this chapter, we will explore techniques for handling social situations and events in a health-conscious and balanced manner.

Plan Ahead:
a. Check the Menu: If you know where you will be dining, review the menu in advance. Look for healthier options or consider making special requests, such as asking for sauces or dressings on the side or substituting certain ingredients.
b. Offer to Contribute: If you're attending a potluck or gathering, offer to bring a healthy dish or side. This ensures that you have a nutritious option available and allows others to enjoy it as well.
c. Eat a Balanced Meal: Prior to attending an event, have a balanced meal or snack that includes protein, healthy fats, and fiber. This can help curb excessive hunger and prevent overindulging later.

Practice Mindful Eating:
a. Be Present: Pay attention to your body's hunger and fullness cues. Before reaching for food, check in with yourself and ask if you are truly hungry or if you are eating out of habit or social pressure.
b. Savor Each Bite: Take your time to appreciate the flavors and textures of the foods you choose to eat. Chew slowly and mindfully, allowing yourself to fully enjoy the experience.
c. Portion Control: Use mindful portioning techniques, such as using a smaller plate, selecting a reasonable serving size, and listening to your body's signals of satisfaction.

Communicate Your Needs:
a. Inform Others: If you have dietary restrictions or preferences, communicate them to your host or the restaurant staff. They may be able to accommodate your needs or provide alternatives.
b. Be Assertive: Don't be afraid to politely decline food offerings that don't align with your health goals. You can simply say, "No, thank you," or offer a brief explanation if necessary.

Seek Support:
a. Recruit an Accountability Partner: Share your health goals and concerns with a trusted friend or family member. They can offer support and help you stay on track during social events.
b. Buddy System: If possible, attend events with someone who shares similar health goals. You can support each other in making mindful choices and hold each other accountable.

Focus on Non-Food Activities:
a. Engage in Conversation: Shift the focus from food to engaging conversations with others. Connect with friends, family, or colleagues, and enjoy the social aspect of the event.
b. Participate in Activities: If the event includes physical activities or games, join in and have fun. This can distract you from solely focusing on food and help burn off some calories as well.

Mindful Indulgences:
a. Choose Wisely: If you want to enjoy a treat or indulge in a favorite dish, make a conscious choice and savor it mindfully. Take a smaller portion, eat it slowly, and fully appreciate the taste.
b. Balanced Approach: Balance indulgences with healthier choices. Fill your plate with mostly nutritious options and allow yourself a smaller portion of the less healthy ones.

Practice Self-Compassion:
a. Avoid Guilt: If you do overindulge or deviate from your usual eating habits during a social event, practice self-compassion and let go of guilt. Remember that occasional deviations do not define your overall progress or well-being.
b. Focus on Progress: Acknowledge the progress you've made in adopting healthier habits and remind yourself that one event or meal does not undo all your efforts.

Remember, social events should be enjoyable experiences. Prioritize your well-being, but also allow yourself to relax and indulge on occasion. Strive for a balanced approach that incorporates healthy choices while still participating in the social aspect of these gatherings. With mindful planning, thoughtful choices, and self-compassion, you can navigate social situations and events while staying true to your health goals.

Healthy Eating on the Go

Choosing Healthy Options at Restaurants and Cafes

Eating out at restaurants and cafes can be enjoyable, but it can also present challenges when it comes to making healthy choices. With some knowledge and strategies, you can navigate the menu and find nutritious options that align with your health goals. In this chapter, we will explore techniques for choosing healthy options at restaurants and cafes.

Review the Menu:
a. Look for Key Indicators: Many menus now highlight healthier options with symbols or labels. Look for keywords like "light," "low-calorie," "vegetarian," or "gluten-free" to identify potentially healthier choices.
b. Scan for Fresh Ingredients: Look for dishes that emphasize fresh fruits, vegetables, lean proteins, whole grains, and minimal added sugars or unhealthy fats.
c. Consider Preparation Methods: Pay attention to the cooking methods used. Opt for grilled, baked, steamed, or roasted options instead of fried or breaded dishes.
d. Customize Your Order: Don't be afraid to ask the server for modifications, such as swapping unhealthy sides for vegetables or requesting dressings and sauces on the side.

Mindful Portions:
a. Share or Split a Dish: Consider sharing a larger entree with a dining companion or asking for a half portion. This can help control portion sizes and reduce the temptation to overeat.
b. Box Up Extras: If the portion size is large, ask for a takeout container at the beginning of the meal and put aside a portion to enjoy later.
c. Avoid Unlimited Offers: Be cautious with all-you-can-eat buffets or bottomless options. These can encourage overeating. Stick to a single serving or opt for a la carte choices instead.

Smart Starters:

a. Opt for Soups and Salads: Begin your meal with a broth-based soup or a salad loaded with vegetables. Choose dressings on the side to control the amount you use.
b. Be Mindful of Appetizers: Select healthier appetizers like grilled vegetables, shrimp cocktail, or hummus with vegetable sticks. Limit deep-fried or cheesy options.

Lean Protein Choices:
a. Choose Lean Meats: Look for options like grilled chicken, turkey, or lean cuts of beef or pork. Avoid breaded or fried proteins.
b. Consider Seafood: Incorporate seafood like salmon, trout, tuna, or shrimp into your meal. They provide omega-3 fatty acids and lean protein.
c. Plant-Based Protein: Explore vegetarian or vegan options that incorporate legumes, tofu, tempeh, or seitan as a protein source.

Whole Grains and Fiber:
a. Seek Whole Grain Alternatives: Opt for whole grain bread, brown rice, quinoa, or whole wheat pasta instead of refined grain options.
b. Add Vegetables: Look for dishes that include a variety of colorful vegetables. They provide fiber, vitamins, and minerals, and can make the meal more satisfying.

Mindful Sides:
a. Choose Smart Side Dishes: Select sides like steamed or roasted vegetables, side salads, or whole grains like quinoa or brown rice. Avoid heavy sides like creamy mashed potatoes or fries.
b. Request Modifications: If a dish comes with unhealthy sides, ask if they can be swapped for healthier alternatives like steamed vegetables or a side salad.

Be Mindful of Sauces and Dressings:
a. Get Sauces on the Side: Ask for sauces, dressings, or gravies to be served on the side. This gives you control over the amount you use and helps limit excess calories, sodium, or unhealthy fats.
b. Opt for Lighter Options: Choose vinaigrettes, salsas, or tomato-based sauces instead of creamy or buttery dressings. These lighter options can still add flavor without excessive calories or unhealthy fats.

Hydration:
a. Choose Water or Unsweetened Beverages: Opt for water, sparkling water, or unsweetened iced tea instead of sugary beverages. If you prefer something flavored, choose infused water or unsweetened herbal teas.

Mindful Desserts:
a. Share a Dessert: If you want to indulge in a dessert, consider sharing it with others to control portion sizes.
b. Fruit-based Options: Look for desserts that feature fresh fruit or fruit-based ingredients. These can provide natural sweetness and additional nutrients.
c. Portion Control: If there are no healthier dessert options available, opt for a small portion or enjoy a few bites to satisfy your craving without overindulging.

Remember, the goal is to make the best possible choices while still enjoying the dining experience. Be flexible and mindful of your preferences and health goals. With practice, you'll become adept at navigating menus, selecting healthier options, and enjoying meals out while prioritizing your well-being.

Eating Well During Travel and Business Trips

Maintaining a healthy diet while traveling or on business trips can be challenging due to unfamiliar surroundings, limited food options, and busy schedules. However, with some planning and strategies in place, it is possible to make nutritious choices and prioritize your well-being. In this chapter, we will explore techniques for eating well during travel and business trips.

Plan Ahead:
a. Research Dining Options: Before your trip, look up restaurants or cafes near your destination that offer healthier choices. Check their menus and reviews to make informed decisions.
b. Pack Healthy Snacks: Bring along portable, non-perishable snacks such as nuts, seeds, dried fruits, protein bars, or whole grain crackers to have on hand when healthy options are limited.
c. Meal Prep: If feasible, prepare some nutritious meals or snacks in advance and pack them in travel-friendly containers. This can help ensure you have healthy options readily available.

Focus on Balanced Meals:
a. Prioritize Protein: Include lean protein sources like grilled chicken, fish, tofu, or legumes in your meals. Protein helps keep you satisfied and supports muscle recovery.
b. Load Up on Vegetables: Seek out salads, vegetable-based dishes, or sides to add nutrients and fiber to your meals.
c. Choose Whole Grains: Opt for whole grain options like whole wheat bread, brown rice, or quinoa to provide sustained energy and fiber.
d. Healthy Fats: Incorporate sources of healthy fats such as avocado, nuts, seeds, or olive oil into your meals. They add flavor and promote satiety.

Smart Restaurant Choices:
a. Navigate the Menu: Look for keywords like "grilled," "steamed," "baked," or "broiled" to identify healthier cooking methods. Avoid fried, breaded, or creamy dishes.
b. Portion Control: Be mindful of portion sizes and consider sharing larger meals or ordering appetizer-sized portions.

c. Customization: Don't hesitate to ask for modifications, such as requesting dressings or sauces on the side or substituting unhealthy sides for steamed vegetables.

Healthy Snacking:
a. Choose Convenient Options: Seek out fresh fruits, cut vegetables, yogurt, or mixed nuts at convenience stores or local markets. These can serve as healthy snacks between meals.
b. Read Labels: If purchasing packaged snacks, read the ingredient lists and nutrition labels to choose options with minimal added sugars, unhealthy fats, or artificial ingredients.

Stay Hydrated:
a. Carry a Reusable Water Bottle: Keep a water bottle with you at all times to stay hydrated throughout your journey. Opt for water instead of sugary beverages or excessive caffeine.
b. Herbal Teas: Pack some herbal tea bags to enjoy in your hotel room or during breaks. They can provide hydration and a soothing beverage option.

Mindful Eating on the Go:
a. Slow Down: Take the time to chew your food thoroughly and savor each bite. This helps with digestion and allows you to be more mindful of your food choices.
b. Mindful Portions: Pay attention to portion sizes and eat until you feel comfortably satisfied, rather than overeating due to distractions or time constraints.
c. Mindful Snacking: When snacking, portion out your snacks rather than eating directly from the package. This helps you be more aware of how much you are consuming.

Prioritize Sleep and Self-Care:
a. Get Sufficient Rest: Aim for adequate sleep to support your overall well-being. This can help regulate hunger hormones and prevent mindless snacking due to fatigue or stress.
b. Manage Stress: Implement stress management techniques, such as deep breathing exercises, meditation, or light exercise, to support your mental and emotional well-being.

Be Flexible and Enjoy Local Cuisine:

a. Embrace Local Flavors: Explore the local cuisine and enjoy new flavors and ingredients. Look for traditional dishes that incorporate wholesome ingredients like fresh produce, lean proteins, and whole grains.
b. Balance Indulgences: It's okay to indulge in local specialties or treats occasionally. Practice moderation and balance by enjoying smaller portions or sharing desserts with others.

Remember, traveling and business trips should be enjoyable experiences. While it may not always be possible to have complete control over your meals, focus on making the best choices available to you and maintaining a balanced approach. By planning ahead, staying mindful of your food choices, and prioritizing self-care, you can eat well and support your well-being even when on the go.

Packing Nutritious Meals for Work and School

Preparing and packing nutritious meals for work and school is an excellent way to support your health goals, save money, and ensure you have access to nourishing options throughout the day. With some planning and creativity, you can pack meals that are delicious, balanced, and satisfying. In this chapter, we will explore techniques for packing nutritious meals for work and school.

Plan and Prep Ahead:
a. Meal Planning: Take some time to plan your meals for the week. Consider your dietary preferences, nutritional needs, and any restrictions or allergies.
b. Batch Cooking: Prepare larger portions of meals and snacks ahead of time. This can include roasting vegetables, cooking grains, or making a large salad to use as a base for different meals throughout the week.
c. Portion Control: Divide your prepared meals into individual containers or portion them into separate bags for easy grab-and-go options.

Balanced Meal Components:
a. Protein Source: Include a lean protein source in your meals, such as grilled chicken, turkey, tofu, beans, or lentils. Protein helps keep you satisfied and supports muscle repair and growth.
b. Whole Grains: Choose whole grain options like brown rice, quinoa, whole wheat bread, or whole grain pasta to provide sustained energy and fiber.
c. Healthy Fats: Incorporate sources of healthy fats like avocados, nuts, seeds, or olive oil. These fats add flavor, provide satiety, and support overall health.
d. Plenty of Fruits and Vegetables: Include a variety of colorful fruits and vegetables for essential vitamins, minerals, and fiber. Opt for fresh produce or prepare pre-cut options to make packing easier.

Packable Meal Ideas:
a. Salads: Prepare a salad with a mix of leafy greens, colorful vegetables, protein (e.g., grilled chicken or chickpeas), and a light dressing. Keep the dressing separate until you're ready to eat to avoid sogginess.

b. Wraps and Sandwiches: Fill whole grain wraps or bread with lean protein, veggies, and a spread like hummus or avocado. Roll them up tightly or use a toothpick to hold them together.
c. Grain Bowls: Assemble a grain bowl using cooked grains (such as quinoa or brown rice), a protein source (e.g., grilled salmon or baked tofu), roasted vegetables, and a flavorful sauce or dressing.
d. Bento Boxes: Use compartmentalized containers to pack a variety of foods, including cut fruits, veggies, whole grain crackers, cheese cubes, and bite-sized protein options like hard-boiled eggs or lean deli meat.
e. Soups and Stews: Prepare a hearty soup or stew in advance and pack it in a thermos. Choose recipes with a good balance of vegetables, lean protein, and whole grains or legumes.
f. Mason Jar Salads: Layer ingredients in a mason jar, starting with dressing at the bottom, followed by sturdy vegetables, proteins, grains, and leafy greens on top. When ready to eat, shake the jar to mix everything together.

Snack and Side Ideas:
a. Fresh Fruit: Pack whole fruits like apples, bananas, or oranges. Alternatively, cut up fruits and store them in portioned containers for easy snacking.
b. Veggie Sticks: Slice raw vegetables like carrots, cucumbers, bell peppers, or celery sticks. Pair them with a hummus or yogurt-based dip for added flavor.
c. Yogurt Parfaits: Layer Greek yogurt with fresh fruits, nuts, and a sprinkle of granola or seeds in a portable container.
d. Trail Mix: Create a custom trail mix using a mix of nuts, seeds, dried fruits, and a few dark chocolate pieces for a sweet treat.
e. Homemade Energy Balls: Make energy balls using ingredients like rolled oats, nut butter, seeds, and a touch of honey or maple syrup. They provide a convenient and satisfying snack option.
f. Hard-Boiled Eggs: Prep a few hard-boiled eggs and store them in the refrigerator for a quick protein-packed snack.

Stay Hydrated:
a. Water Bottle: Carry a reusable water bottle to stay hydrated throughout the day. Consider infusing it with fruits or herbs for added flavor.

b. Herbal Teas: Pack some herbal tea bags to enjoy during breaks or to have a warm beverage option.

Storage and Safety:
a. Insulated Lunch Bags or Coolers: Invest in an insulated lunch bag or cooler to keep your packed meals and snacks fresh and at a safe temperature.
b. Ice Packs: Use reusable ice packs to keep perishable items cool and prevent food spoilage.
c. Safe Food Handling: Ensure that you follow proper food safety practices, including washing hands before handling food, storing perishable items at appropriate temperatures, and reheating meals thoroughly if needed.

Variety and Enjoyment:
a. Rotate Recipes: Keep your meals interesting by rotating recipes and trying new flavor combinations. This helps prevent boredom and keeps you motivated to stick to your packed meals.
b. Treat Yourself: Include a small treat or indulgence in your packed meals occasionally. This can be a square of dark chocolate, a homemade healthy dessert, or a small portion of your favorite snack.

Remember, the key to successful meal packing is planning, preparation, and creativity. Experiment with different recipes, flavors, and textures to keep your meals enjoyable and satisfying. By packing nutritious meals, you'll be fueling your body with nourishing foods and setting yourself up for success throughout the work or school day.

Conclusion

Recap and Key Principles of Healthy Eating

Balanced Meals: Aim for balanced meals that include a variety of food groups. Incorporate lean proteins, whole grains, fruits, vegetables, and healthy fats into your daily diet.

Portion Control: Be mindful of portion sizes and listen to your body's hunger and fullness cues. Avoid overeating and practice portion control to maintain a healthy weight.

Nutrient Density: Choose foods that are nutrient-dense, meaning they provide a high amount of nutrients relative to their calorie content. Focus on whole, minimally processed foods to maximize nutritional value.

Moderation: Practice moderation when it comes to indulgent or less nutritious foods. It's okay to enjoy treats occasionally, but balance them with healthier options and control portion sizes.

Mindful Eating: Engage in mindful eating practices by slowing down, savoring each bite, and paying attention to your body's hunger and fullness cues. This helps you develop a healthier relationship with food and enhances your eating experience.

Hydration: Stay adequately hydrated by drinking water throughout the day. Limit sugary beverages and opt for water, herbal tea, or unsweetened drinks instead.

Meal Planning and Preparation: Plan and prepare meals ahead of time to ensure you have nutritious options readily available. This helps you make healthier choices and avoid relying on less nutritious convenience foods.

Variety and Moderation: Aim for a variety of foods to ensure you get a wide range of nutrients. Embrace different flavors, textures, and cooking methods to keep your meals interesting and enjoyable.

Whole Foods: Choose whole, unprocessed foods whenever possible. They are typically higher in nutrients, fiber, and antioxidants compared to highly processed foods.

Flexibility and Individualization: Recognize that everyone's nutritional needs and preferences are unique. Adapt healthy eating principles to fit your individual needs, cultural background, and personal tastes.

Remember, healthy eating is a lifelong journey, and it's important to find a sustainable approach that works for you. Focus on nourishing your body with wholesome foods, practicing moderation, and maintaining a positive mindset towards food and eating. By incorporating these key principles into your daily life, you can achieve and maintain a balanced and healthy diet.

Inspiration and Motivation for Sustaining a Healthy Lifestyle

Set Clear Goals: Define your health and wellness goals, whether it's improving your physical fitness, managing a chronic condition, or achieving a healthy weight. Having clear goals gives you something to work towards and helps keep you motivated.

Find Your "Why": Identify the underlying reasons why a healthy lifestyle is important to you. It could be to have more energy, feel confident in your body, reduce the risk of disease, or be a positive role model for your loved ones. Understanding your personal motivations can help you stay committed to your healthy choices.

Celebrate Small Victories: Recognize and celebrate the small achievements along your journey towards a healthy lifestyle. Whether it's choosing a nutritious meal, completing a workout, or making a positive behavior change, every step forward is worth acknowledging.

Surround Yourself with Support: Seek out a supportive network of friends, family, or like-minded individuals who share your goals or encourage your healthy choices. Having a support system can provide motivation, accountability, and inspiration during challenging times.

Educate Yourself: Stay informed about the benefits of a healthy lifestyle through books, articles, podcasts, or reputable online sources. Understanding the positive impact of healthy choices on your overall well-being can inspire you to maintain a healthy lifestyle.

Explore New Activities: Keep your healthy lifestyle exciting and enjoyable by trying new activities and exercise routines. Explore different types of exercises, such as yoga, hiking, swimming, or dance classes, to find activities that you genuinely enjoy.

Reward Yourself: Treat yourself to non-food rewards for reaching milestones or sticking to your healthy habits. It could be buying new workout gear, taking a relaxing spa day, or indulging in a hobby you love. Rewards can provide extra motivation and a sense of accomplishment.

Practice Self-Care: Prioritize self-care activities that nourish your mind, body, and spirit. Engage in activities like meditation, mindfulness, journaling, or spending quality time with loved ones. Taking care of yourself holistically enhances your motivation to maintain a healthy lifestyle.

Reflect on Progress: Regularly assess and reflect on the progress you've made. Look back at how far you've come and the positive changes you've implemented. This reflection can serve as a reminder of your capabilities and inspire you to continue on your healthy path.

Be Kind to Yourself: Remember that maintaining a healthy lifestyle is a journey with ups and downs. Embrace imperfections and be kind to yourself when faced with setbacks or challenges. Treat yourself with compassion, and use setbacks as opportunities to learn and grow.

By staying inspired and motivated, you can sustain a healthy lifestyle that brings you joy, vitality, and long-term well-being. Keep your goals in mind, surround yourself with support, and find fulfillment in the positive changes you make. Embrace the journey, and remember that each day is an opportunity to live your healthiest life.

Printed in Great Britain
by Amazon